Pretend Play
Among 3-Year-Olds

Pretend Play
Among 3-Year-Olds

Edited by
Mira Stambak
Hermina Sinclair
University of Geneva

English translation by
Hermina and Morris Sinclair
from the French
Les Jeux de Fiction entre Enfants de 3 Ans

LEA **LAWRENCE ERLBAUM ASSOCIATES, PUBLISHERS**
1993 **Hillsdale, New Jersey**   **Hove and London**

Originally published by Presses Universitaires de France
Copyright © 1990

Lawrence Erlbaum Associates, Inc., Publishers
365 Broadway
Hillsdale, New Jersey 07642

Library of Congress Cataloging-in-Publication Data

Jeux de fiction entre enfants de 3 ans. English.
    Pretend play among 3-year olds / edited by Mira Stambak, Hermina
Sinclair ; English translation by Hermina and Morris Sinclair.
        p.   cm.
    Includes bibliographical references.
    ISBN 0-8058-1243-1
    1. Symbolic play.   2. Symbolism (Psychology) in children.
3. Imagination in children.   4. Social interaction in children.
5. Symbolic play—Case studies.   6. Symbolism (Psychology) in
children—Case studies.   7. Imagination in children—Case studies.
8. Social interaction in children—Case studies.   I. Stambak, Mira.
II. Sinclair, Hermina.   III. Title.
BF717.J4913   1993
155.42 '38—dc20   92-28297
                                                                         CIP

Books published by Lawrence Erlbaum Associates are printed on acid-free
paper, and their bindings are chosen for strength and durability.

Printed in the United States of America
10   9   8   7   6   5   4   3   2   1

Contents

Introduction*

Hermina Sinclair
Université de Genève

Mira Stambak
Institut National de Recherche Pédagogique, Paris

The four studies of collective pretend play among 3-year-old children present-ed in this book were carried out by a number of researchers who share a theo-retical background, who use the same methods, and who have worked together for many years.

From the outset, our studies were based on observations of children acting, not in a laboratory setting, but in an environment with which they were familiar (i.e., the day-care center or kindergarten they frequented). We became aware that the observation of children acting spontaneously—in the presence of adults who rarely intervene, but who show that they are interested in the children's activity—contributed to our knowledge of various aspects of development. Videotapes of spontaneous activities, recorded in different situations and then transcribed and analyzed via similar methods, often revealed capacities of very young children that are rarely referred to in the literature (cf. Sinclair, Stam-bak, Lézine, Rayna, & Verba, 1982/1989; Stambak et al., 1983). It also be-came clear that different types of play objects often led to different types of activities, and that it thus was illuminating to vary the material conditions. Gradually, we also became aware of the need for collaboration between research-ers and caretakers or educators.

Our theoretical framework of reference is that provided by Piaget's con-structivism and interactionism. Piagetian theory considers the subject to be

---

*Translators' note: In references with two dates separated by a slash, the first gives the year of original publication, the second that of the English translation. Quotations have been taken whenever possible from the published English version.

active in the construction of knowledge, and to progress cognitively by transforming the relations with the world of objects as well as with the world of
people—not as an organism that acts only in reaction to stimuli provided by
the environment. This interaction leads to progressive construction, whereby
new acquisitions are integrated into already existing knowledge, either by further elaboration or by a reorganization of existing knowledge. According to
Piaget, one of the important mechanisms of progress is that of abstraction,
which, especially in the first years of life, consists in detaching from its immediate context an already well-installed activity, still closely linked to a precise moment in time and a precise location in space, thus opening up possibilities
for conceptualization.

One of our first studies (Sinclair et al., 1982/1989) concerned children between the ages of 1 and 2, acting individually on various types of objects in
the presence of an interested, but nonintervening adult. Clearly, the children's
activities were often derived from interactions they had had with others or from
what they had seen other people, frequently adults, do (e.g., using a brush
on the carpet). In our later research, social interaction, and more specifically
peer interaction, hitherto rarely investigated in very young children, became
our main object of study.

In his epistemological and psychological theory, Piaget emphasized the importance of interaction between persons who consider themselves equal. He
stated that knowledge becomes objectivized only when it is shared with others,
and that the necessity of sharing and cooperating is the same at all levels of
development, including that of scientific research: objective knowledge is acquired only when "it has been verified (and not simply accepted) by other in-
vestigators" (Piaget, 1965b/1971, p. 12). Thus, it is only when our models
or systems correspond to those of others that they can lead to further progress.
Sharing ideas, discussing and arguing, or more simply playing together are
essential ingredients in the construction of knowledge at all ages. Knowledge
acquisition is in fact a co-construction in collaboration:

> without interchange of thought and cooperation with others, the individual would
> never come to group his operations into a coherent whole: in this sense, there-
> fore, operational grouping presupposes social life. But, on the other hand, actual
> exchanges of thought obey a law of equilibrium which again could only be an
> operational grouping, since to cooperate is also to coordinate operations. The
> grouping is therefore a form of equilibrium of interindividual actions as well as
> individual actions, and it thus regains its autonomy at the very core of social life.
> (Piaget, 1965a, pp. 174–175)

Although Piaget rarely studied interaction between individuals, he considered such interaction to play a constructive part in cognitive development. In
La Construction du Réel Chez l'Enfant (Piaget, 1937/1954), the chapter on the development of causality includes a section on "causality through imitation"

(p. 249 sqq) and his analysis of infants' actions reported in this section leads him to note "it is therefore very probable. . .that contact with persons plays an essential role in the processes of objectification and externalization" (p. 252). In *Le Langage et la Pensée Chez l'Enfant* (1923, 3rd rev. ed. 1948/1959, p. 250), Piaget remarked that what he called "genuine dialogues," implying discussion and cooperation, appear earlier (before the age of 4) and are also more frequent in exchanges between children than between children and adults. "Not only are exchanges with information more numerous between children, but the information is of a more evolved type. . . . It seems as though the conflict of opinions and intentions opened up a channel for discussion on a higher plane" (1948/1959, p. 246). Unfortunately, it was the notion of "egocentric language," as it was treated in that book, which principally retained the attention of psychologists; although Piaget clearly stated (1948/1959, p. 261) that he was interested in instances where children speak without trying to act on interlocutors and without distinguishing between their own and the point of view of others, he also stated that "socialized language comes no doubt as early as speech itself." Nonetheless, Piaget considered genuine discussion between children to be rare before the age of 4 and he did not study the development of this type of interaction.

Our observations in child-care centers led to our first studies on peer interaction with toddlers in their second year of life (Stambak et al., 1983). We were particularly interested in the role such interaction might play in cognitive development. Our analyses of the communicative and cognitive activities of these children, observed when playing in small groups with the objects at their disposal, showed that they often center their attention on the same idea of what can be done with the objects. Analyzing how these activities unfolded (until the group dispersed or passed on to doing something else) we came to distinguish two types of interaction that appeared to further the acquisition of knowledge.

On the one hand, the children adopt one another's ideas of possible actions and repeat them on the objects they happen to have taken up, whereupon they elaborate the actions further. The repeats are not simple imitations because they are carried out on similar, although not identical objects, or produce the same result by different means (e.g., putting a stick through a wooden ring, and piercing a little ball of modeling clay with a stick; taking several objects out of a box by hand, and emptying a box by turning it over). The children thus show detachment from specific situations and the beginnings of abstraction; the child whose idea was taken up by another as well as the child who took it up are now in the presence of a situation that could not arise had the actions been performed by one child alone. In the first place, the child who initiated the sequence now observes the action as it were from the outside, which, in our opinion, facilitates a detachment from one's own activity as well as a separation between action and object: Both are ingredients of the objectivation of knowledge. In the second place, the children observe the two activities almost simultaneously, which provides greater opportunity for discovering relationships between the particularities of the actions and their effects on the objects than when the same actions are carried out (necessarily in succession) by one child.

On the other hand, the 2-year-olds may start playing together with the same objects. They may decide to put small toys into the same box, or they may start pretend play, as when one child plays at feeding another. Certain types of play can be pursued only with a partner, such as object exchanges or hide-and-seek. This necessity leads to an awareness of new problems: A partner has to be found and an agreement reached on what kind of play is to be shared. At this very early age, we observed genuine preverbal negotiations during which the children communicate their intentions and clarify their ideas to a partner who tries to understand them. Once an agreement to play a certain game is reached, early forms of collaboration can be observed: Each partner in turn elaborates the proposal of the other in order to keep the shared activity going. These nonverbal negotiations sometimes lead to conflicting ideas and desires, but such disagreements are often resolved by strategies that attest an already well-developed social intelligence. Our observations thus reveal various capacities, hitherto underestimated at this age, particularly a capacity for interpersonal coordination, which plays an important part in the acquisition of knowledge.

Thought, in contrast to practical intelligence, operates with signifiers or symbols, and becomes gradually detached from immediate perceptions and actions in the here and now. Just as during the sensorimotor period, action schemes become organized into systems, symbols (in the broad sense of mental representations) also become organized into systems, especially into collective systems (e.g., natural languages, number systems, maps, etc.). We therefore decided to pursue our observational studies in the same situation using the same methods of analysis with children whose representative thought is in full spate of development (i.e., between the ages of 2 and 4).

Like many other authors, we considered that pretend play opens a particularly interesting window of observation onto young children's knowledge. In pretend play, children create symbols by their imaginative use of objects, their actions, gestures, postures and verbalizations, and combine these different behaviors in coordinated symbolizations; symbol creation and combination are two fundamental capacities that underlie human thinking. Symbol construction is a manifestation of cognitive capacities as well as a condition for their development. When Piaget studied rule games (1932/1932) and symbolic play (1945/1951), he focused his analyses and interpretations on the close link between thought and its representational foundations: In both studies he used his results to specify the characteristics of what he then called "intuitive" or "symbolic" thought of children between the ages of 2 and 7.

Several authors (e.g., Bruner, 1972) mentioned that, in play in general and pretend play in particular, one can observe not only the construction of symbols and conventions but also, more generally, a detachment from present spatiotemporal reality. Such freedom from spatiotemporal constraints is of course a characteristic of human language, and several authors have drawn a parallel between the acquisition of language and the beginnings of symbolic play (McCune-Nicolich 1981; Piaget 1945/1951; Vygotsky 1967, and others). But it is equally important to view this detachment from the immediate situation as a feature that distinguishes sensorimotor intelligence from thought. According to Piaget, sensorimotor intelligence is directed by the desire to reach a particular goal via an action and to discover new properties in the physical or social world; thought (from the end of the sensorimotor period onward) adds to this centration a desire for understanding, a focus on the why and how of the success or failure of practical actions. This detachment from the immediate context has yet other characteristics: It makes it possible to see a particular problem as an example of a more general one; similarly, Piaget considered that the capacity to imagine new possibilities is an essential characteristic of cognitive development.

In this perspective, it is possible to specify how the observation of pretend play provides opportunities for apprehending young children's knowledge in various domains.

1. The absence of material constraints in pretend play allows the observation of children's knowing-how and knowing-that before they can make such knowledge explicit. For example, Piaget (1945/1951, obs. 81) described how J. (2;5) pretends to prepare her younger sister's bath: She takes a blade of grass to serve as a thermometer and a big box as a bathtub, and announces the presence of water verbally. She plunges the thermometer into the bath, looks at it, finds the water too hot, waits a moment, puts the thermometer back into the water and says: *It's O.K. Goody!* It is unlikely that at her age she could really have prepared a bath or even helped to get it ready (cf. the difficulties in Example 3, following). But she clearly knows a lot about it; she knows what a thermometer is used for and she also knows that it is a precious instrument to be handled with care, because at the end she puts the blade of grass carefully into a box. Her knowledge could only be shown in pretend play, not in real life.

2. The absence of a focus on actions leading to an observable goal also makes it possible to gain insight into children's socioaffective knowledge. Piaget (1945/1951, obs. 81) reported that J. (2;1), when playing at feeding her doll, speaks to the doll just as her mother speaks to her in order to get her to continue eating: *Another little drop. To please Jacqueline. Eat another little bit.* J. shows that she has interiorized the situation in which she re-

fuses food while she is being encouraged to eat more. She is not reproducing the adult's utterances in a real situation in which she would try to make a real baby eat. Her doll does not eat anything, nor does the doll refuse to eat, thus no observable behavior elicits her encouraging talk and no observable effect follows it.

3. As has often been remarked, pretend play may involve the theatrical production of emotionally charged scenes and allow observation of the means used by children to resolve personal conflict. Piaget (1945/1951, obs. 84) reported how J. (3;11) was not allowed to go into the kitchen where pails of hot water were standing in preparation for a bath. J. said: *Well, then I'll go into a pretend kitchen! Once I saw a little boy who went into a kitchen, and when Odette came with the hot water, he went to the side.* J. continued on this theme, compensating for her frustration, and finished with symbolic acceptance: *So he didn't go to the kitchen any more.* The boy imagined by J. first showed that the adults who stopped him from going near the hot water were wrong: he knew very well not to get too close. J. herself was not given the opportunity to demonstrate this know-how; by inventing the little boy story she denied that the interdiction was justified and nevertheless complied symbolically.

Such features of pretend play are found in individual as well as in collective play. In individual play, however, the child can attribute symbolic meanings to objects and actions without specification or justification. In collective play by contrast, symbolic meanings as well as the theme and elaboration of the fiction must be shared between partners, for the success of collective fiction depends on the coherence and duration of the scenes constructed together; and this calls for harmony between the partners' ideas and desires. Collective pretend play thus allows us to study reciprocal adaptations via explanations and arguments on which the equilibrated exchange of thought between equals depends. In Piaget's theory, this type of discussion is as essential to the construction of objective knowledge as is the equilibrium between assimilation and accommodation to an individual's successful interaction with the world of objects. The study of collective pretend play thus provides opportunities for observing not only young children's knowledge, but also their capacities for constructing equilibrated exchanges of thought. The characteristics of such exchanges were defined by Piaget (1965a, p. 162) with reference to children of say 6 or 7 onward. Grice (1975), in his maxims for adult discussion, provided similar formulations. For Piaget, the three following characteristics are essential:

1. The partners possess a common framework of reference, a shared system of symbols and definitions, in the sense that they do not exclusively use personal symbols and subjective meanings.

2. The partners show that they do not abandon propositions that have been

accepted as valid. This "conservation of propositions" is genuine only if it is the result of a common accord, not when one partner imposes constraints authoritatively.

3. The partners show reciprocity of thought: "their discussion results in shared propositions or in distinct, but reciprocal propositions that can be coordinated."

In our view, the four studies published in this book confirm the hypothesized privileged status of spontaneous collective pretend play for our understanding of the thinking of young children as well as the special interest of the age of 3. The variety of observational situations (in the familiar surroundings of the day-care center but sometimes in the playground and in the presence of different objects) brought to light several, often unsuspected aspects of sociocognitive development. Without going into details, we can describe some of the findings and explain why they were interesting from our point of view.

All of the contributors noted many of the themes described by others: excursions, picnics, birthday parties, and other events in the children's daily lives. As has often been pointed out, such play episodes show the children's knowledge of social events; but we consider the enactment of such themes to have a favorable influence on cognitive development in general. At the age of 3, children are able to function symbolically via the use of language, and also via the attribution of symbolic meanings to objects and actions. This representational ability allows them to play everyday scenes in an abbreviated form, focusing on essential moments. Such temporal compression provides opportunities for the children to apprehend logical, causal, and spatiotemporal relations between activities without the constraints of physical objects and of actions that must be carried out in succession over a certain time. Moreover, this representation is shared; it requires and allows the children to construct explicit links with the past (they often remind one another of an already enacted event) as well as with the future (they propose further developments of the theme). In their schematic, temporally compressed reproductions of familiar events, the children thus show more than their social knowledge; a network of various temporal and causal relations is activated, partly constructed during the play episode itself.

In chapters 1 and 2, the absence of toys that suggest particular themes and symbolic uses (such as cups, plates, combs, dolls, etc.) led the children to construct a shared system of meanings for the symbolic transformation of objects. The children were aware that they needed to establish shared meanings for objects such as small blocks, wooden bars, and the like, if these were to be used in pretend play. They understood that "neutral" objects lend themselves to multiple symbolic uses (each object on its own, or in combination with another object) and in certain episodes, described in chapter 1, they transform the attribution of meanings to the objects into the theme of the play itself. Each partner makes it clear that an object is treated as if it were something else; the partners often take turns doing this (as in a dialogue), but without creating a scenario or a narrative. In other episodes, the shared system of reference serves to link the various elements of the play theme. The children communicate, often at length, about the imaginary activity to be acted out: A plan is suggested in action or expressed verbally; if necessary, roles are given to the partners, which sometimes leads to negotiations; and their various ideas are clarified and confirmed. The theme and its elaboration are worked out while the fiction is being acted, just as when adult actors engage in improvisation, and this demands a certain removal from one's own pretend actions. The children thus construct the common reference framework that is indispensable for interindividual coordination and the elaboration of the scenario. The strategies by which such shared symbolic frameworks are constructed depend to a large extent on the familiarity of the theme. The analysis of the processes leading to the construction of the framework in different situations brings to light various modalities by which the condition for equilibrated exchanges of thought is brought about.

In chapter 2, which concerns pretend-play episodes in the day-care playground, the authors observed that certain symbolic frameworks were conserved in time and in space by a large number of children and that they served for a variety of pretend-play themes. Such propagation of symbols and rules for pretend play may well be an important constructive factor in the establishment of a sort of microculture within a community of children.

In chapter 3, which describes the activities of small groups playing with a doll and some toy kitchen utensils, the objects at the children's disposal have their own symbolic and social meaning, and it was thus not necessary to construct a reference frame. In this situation, the children are preoccupied with other aspects of their interactions during pretend play. According to Bateson (1955), play in such a situation has two levels, one concerning communication between partners in their fictional roles (mother, baby, etc.), and the other concerning communication between the partners themselves as individuals with their own personality, affinities, and moods. In this chapter, particular attention is paid to the socioaffective aspects of pretend play.

Chapter 4 shows other facets of collective pretend play. The observations were made in a day-care center where the caretakers were interested in puppets, and occasionally gave shows for the children. The episodes reported concern occasions where the children themselves were the puppet masters. The analysis reveals yet other types of knowledge elaborated by children. Their capacity to assimilate the general features of a puppet show (presentation of characters, ways of soliciting the audience's attention, etc.), after having assisted as spectators at only a few shows, are quite astonishing. They immediately entered into the interpersonal relations between the puppet actors. The partners attributed roles to their puppets and staged characters who have similar status (e.g., two friends, two teachers) as well as characters who have complementary status (e.g., teacher–pupil, aggressor–victim). The interaction between these characters may be conflictual, making the show dramatic. In dramatic scenes, the children manifest their already well-developed knowledge of the kind of relations that may exist, relations that they may have experienced themselves, or observed between others. They also show their knowledge of rules of behavior governing daily life. They distinguish serious transgressions from less serious ones; they know what "crimes" should be punished, and know that the seriousness of the punishment should correspond to the seriousness of the crime. This kind of knowledge often appears in what the children say about the actions they have the puppets perform: They comment upon the events. Just as in the case of knowledge of interindividual relations, we must conclude that their knowledge of the rules of social behavior goes beyond simple know-how. A certain interiorization must have taken place: At earlier ages, children can already behave in real-life situations according to certain social rules and can even foresee reproaches that may follow certain transgressions; but to be able to create fictional situations and to envisage both the role of somebody who judges the behavior of others (usually an adult) and the role of the one who is judged is evidence of knowledge at a higher level.

The importance of analyzing the processes of reciprocal adjustment observed in the different types of collective pretend play needs to be stressed. In all four studies, the authors observed moments when the children tried to come to an agreement, either at the outset or in the course of play. At these times, the children negotiate and show their capacities for mutual adjustment most clearly. They endeavor to conciliate two apparently contradictory desires: that of using the many possibilities in pretend play for developing a theme that pleases each of them personally, and that of having the particular satisfaction of developing a theme together. Sometimes the negotiations are stormy and nearly bring the action to a close. But generally, as in almost all the examples given, the children manage to resolve their conflict and to come to an agreement. Subtle strategies are used to convince partners to accept this or that idea. Sometimes, however, the ideas proposed are not understood. This does not necessarily prevent further elaboration of the play: The children already know how to ask for clarification, and the child whose idea was not understood may be able to be more explicit.

The duration and emotional tone of the negotiations appear to differ according to the type of play. When there are external constraints (such as the necessity to keep the audience amused during a puppet show) negotiations are brief and efficient. The children appear to be aware that the situation requires a quick solution. By contrast, when pretend roles with a clear affective connotation have to be distributed (e.g., who will be the mother, and who the baby) negotiations may become conflictual. This seems to happen often when the children communicate on two different levels, as shown by Schwartzman (1978),

Forbes, Maxwell-Katz, and Paul (1986), following Bateson (1955). Each utterance conveys a double meaning: a proposition within the play and a message to the partner as a real person in order to bring about a change in his
or her way of behaving.

The strong desire of children to continue to play together leads them to search
for a solution to such conflicts as may arise. Because of the fictional character
of the play, the children can experiment with relations they cannot experience
in real life, and they can remove themselves from the emotional impact of confrontations with others. In this way, the process of differentiation between the
self and the other, as studied by Wallon (1949), may be consolidated.

The process of differentiation of self and other on the emotional plane is
parallel to the gradual (although never complete) disappearance of egocentrism
in the Piagetian sense. "Social egocentrism" is the term coined by Piaget for
the period when there is confusion or even fusion between the child's own point
of view and that of others (Piaget, 1923, reprinted 1948/1959 p. 267 sqq), and
when the child's own thoughts are felt to be common to all because escape
from subjectivity is not yet possible (Piaget, 1926/1929. p. 276).

The recent interest in what is called the *child's theory of mind* (cf. Butterworth,
1991); that is children's ideas about the thoughts, beliefs, desires, emotions
of themselves and of others, and especially the question when and on what
evidence one can credit children with a coherent naive theory of mind seems
to be a new elaboration of Piaget's theories on egocentrism and its decrease
between the ages of 3 and 6. Interestingly, the crucial tasks whose successful
completion are supposed to mark the child's very first theory of mind seem
to show that, before the age of 4, children behave exactly according to Piaget's
description of one of the characteristics of egocentrism: Children believe that
their thoughts and knowledge are common to all. The experiments all concern
situations where one person has a different belief from the child subject, a belief that is in contradiction with the child's correct knowledge. For example,
a story is acted out for the child in which a girl puts a toy in a certain place
and then departs. In her absence, another child hides the toy in a different
place. The girl returns and the subject is asked to show where the girl is going
to look for her toy. Almost all 3-year-olds and a good many 4-year-olds said
the girl is going to look in the place where *they* know the toy is hidden, not
where the girl put it originally. 3-year-olds do not seem to understand how
someone can believe anything other than what they know to be the truth. Our
observations may have a certain relevance to this issue. The capacity to attribute beliefs to others, especially beliefs contrary to one's own and to reality,
is not supposed to appear all of a sudden in full-fledged form, but to grow out
of earlier aptitudes, about which little is known. Without going so far as to
suggest that, in certain scenes reported in chapters 3 and 4, the children spontaneously create situations similar to the erroneous-belief experiments, the
paradoxes reported in chapter 3 and some of the "tease sequences" in chapter

4 seem to indicate that our 3-year-old subjects are already capable of predict-
ing someone else's behavior arising from an erroneous belief.

Discussions and interpersonal adjustments are equally important from a Piagetian point of view. They prepare the critical and objective attitude needed
for the acquisition of objective knowledge, made possible by the operatory systems that "necessarily combine to form a system of cooperation which is both
logical and social" (Piaget, 1948/1959, p. 281). This system of logical and social cooperation underlies equilibrated exchanges of thought, the characteristics of which were previously outlined. In the four chapters of this book,
3-year-old children are shown to be constructing the type of discussion among
equals, the importance of which for cognitive development was stressed by Piaget. They are already able to conserve the themes they have agreed upon and
they accept the reciprocity of propositions after negotiation and explicit com-
promises. Social interaction and especially peer interaction thus seem, at a far
earlier age than is generally supposed, to prepare the principal characteristics
of the main reasoning principles brought to light by Piaget with reference to
the ages of 6 or 7.

Several authors have wondered whether collective pretend play can contribute to intellectual development. According to one hypothesis, originally proposed by Mead (1934) and taken up by Bateson (1955) and Golomb and
Cornelius (1977), the constructive power of pretend play stems from the fact
that the child who pretends to be a different person (or sometimes an animal)
conserves personal identity and is able to abandon the assumed role in order
to make remarks and comments in his or her own name. Similarly, the child
can confer symbolic meaning on an object, but remain perfectly aware of the
normal use of this object and return to the normal use from time to time. A
certain kind of reversibility can thus already be observed at an early age in
pretend play. Golomb and Cornelius (1977) carried out a learning experiment
during which children between the ages of 4 and 4½ played with an ex-
perimenter who occasionally stepped out of the fictional frame and asked the
children questions designed to make them aware of this duality of persons and
objects. A control group and the experimental group both passed a pretest on
the conservation of liquids and of substance (before the learning sessions); com-
pared to the control group, the experimental group showed surprisingly good
progress on the conservation posttests. An exact duplication of the experiment,
however, failed to yield the same results, which indeed were surprising at the
ages studied. Nonetheless, in a general sense, the hypothesis of a positive influence of duality in pretend play on the elaboration of operatory thought cannot be dismissed out of hand. As we have argued, however, another aspect
of collective pretend play may well exert such an influence (i.e., the nature
of the exchanges between the children). The negotiations, justifications, and
proposals of compromise observed show that at the age of our subjects the cor-
respondences and reciprocities that, according to Piaget (1948/1959, p. 281)

''constitute the most important grouping'' are being constructed during the interactions.

From this point of view, the characteristics of peer interaction between young children would not only be clearly observable during collective pretend play, but would exert a positive influence on the children's sociocognitive development, as much as, or possibly even more than, the detachment from the *hic et nunc* and the comprehension of the duality of fictional roles stressed by other authors.

Chapter 1

Construction and Sharing of Meanings in Pretend Play Among Young Children*

Mina Verba
Université René Descartes, Paris

The study of pretend play among young children has been receiving increasing attention in recent years (cf. overviews by Bretherton, 1984; Fein, 1981; Hutt, Tyler, Hutt, & Christopherson, 1989). Many studies have focused on communication among peers during pretend play and the possible role of communication in cognitive and social development. Pretend play is considered a preferential terrain for the study of mutual understanding and negotiation among preschool aged children. Because shared pretend play is a collaborative activity, it implies the construction of shared meanings underlying the necessary coordinations between participants. Objects, actions, and persons are symbolically transformed in pretend play to take on meanings other than those they have ordinarily, and the partners have to construct a common frame of reference. This chapter is concerned with the construction of shared symbolic meanings in dyadic play at the age of 3.

All communication takes place within a context of established meanings that allow for mutual comprehension. In verbal communication, partners rely on conventional, socially established meanings, but during pretend play that is often not possible because a fiction is created that suspends material and social reality. Children construct arbitrary and subjective links between objects and events, they may inverse time sequences and alter generally accepted rules, but they have to take their partners into account, for without them no playing together would be possible. A shared framework of meanings has thus to be

---

*This chapter is based on observations made in a day-care center in Paris.

constructed within which mutual comprehension of make-believe scenes, roles, and actions can take place. As proposed by Piaget (1965a; cf. Introduction), one of the characteristics of an equilibrated exchange of thought (necessary for all progress in knowledge) resides in the establishment of precisely such a framework. Many kinds of social exchanges precede the capacity to establish shared meanings, and the study of pretend play can here provide some particularly interesting insights. Each partner in a pretend-play episode brings to the interaction ideas and meanings that may be derived from individual experience and that have to be reciprocally adjusted. Each child has to find expressions for thoughts and intentions so that the partner can join in and contribute to the fiction. Conventions have to be established to enable each partner to interpret what the other says and does. The schema in Fig. 1.1 presents the general characteristics of such shared-meaning systems.

Individual meanings (spaces A and B) are expressed during the interaction, and generate an intermediate space where each child adjusts his or her own thinking to that of the other (spaces A^1 and B^1). Through various ways of informing, explaining, clarifying, and negotiating, the individual meanings are harmonized and inserted into a shared-meaning system (space AB). This system underlies the exchanges and facilitates further sharing.

Among the first to study shared meaning systems in play activities of young children, Brenner and Mueller (1982) observed peer interactions among 18-month-old boys and showed how they came to share play themes such as follow the leader and hide-and-seek, and how the construction of shared meanings contributed to their play. Musatti and Panni (1981), Verba (1982), and Stambak and Verba (1986) also studied the social play of infants in the second year of life (i.e., in the preverbal period), and showed that infants used various means (gestures, actions on objects, facial expressions, directed gazing, and vocalizing) to express wishes or agreement. The establishment of shared meanings allows for a smooth sequence of interindividual activities. Efforts to communicate symbolic meanings during pretend play without the use of language were also observed at this age. In particular, the infants used emphatic movements (e.g., throwing the head far back when pretending to drink from a cup and inviting another child to take part in the pretense), and facial expressions (e.g., smiling) to signal the nonliteral meaning of an activity.

Many researchers have studied verbal communication in role-play among older children. Various communication processes for coordinating partners' activities were brought to light, and are used while the children are playing their roles, or take the form of comments when they temporarily step out of the play frame (cf. Franklin, 1981; Garvey & Berndt, 1977; Giffin, 1984). The first to study the construction of meaning in the totality of a pretend episode were Forbes et al. (1986), who concerned themselves with the way symbolic actions, roles, and transformations of objects are integrated into the various phases of the sequence. The analyses carried out by these authors highlight

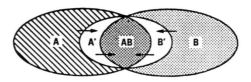

FIG. 1.1.   A–B personal meanings. A'–B' social interactions. AB shared-meaning system.

the negotiations that, pursued by their 5-year-old subjects, led to a system of meanings within which the various pretend actions were understood and coordinated by the partners.

Researchers agree that, from the first appearance of social play to the apogee of the pretend-play period, the coordination of symbolic activities is only possible if the participants share the fictional character of the play situation and understand the meanings attributed to the various events, characters, and objects. Yet it remains an open question how exactly interaction among children during pretend play brings about the sharing of meanings. Our analyses of the data obtained with 3-year-olds are based on an approach to collective pretend play that considers this activity to be a complex totality of various components, including social interactions. In pretend play, children use both cognitive and social abilities, as well as their individual emotional experiences. The simple fact of collective play bears witness to their wanting to be together and to act together in a way that makes sense. Reciprocal socioaffective links are established and imagined events are acted within a common theme. Choice of theme depends on desires and interests appropriate to the age of the children and their mental representations. But each participant has individual wishes and intentions, and only the desire to play together can override these obstacles to collaboration. The desire for common play activity leads to negotiations, as well as to concessions when disagreements occur. The desire to collaborate and the need for coherence govern collective pretend play, which is not subject to external conventional rules nor to the constraints of material reality. Reciprocal adjustments are necessary at each of the three levels that can be distinguished (cf. Verba, 1985): (a) imagining a content for the activity, (b) sharing it with a partner or partners, and (c) managing the pretense once it gets going.

Imagining a Content.   The imaginative creation of a fictional content makes demands on various mental activities. On the one hand, symbolic transformations have to be carried out on objects (a familiar object is given a different status), on persons (the children pretend to be other persons or animals), on space (a corner of the playroom becomes a forest, a beach, etc.), and on time (*Now it's time for dinner!*). These transformations depend on a particular cognitive activity. On the other hand, ideas have to be elaborated to create a "story," and to attribute appropriate characteristics to the players and the situation. These ideas, in order to be described (verbally or in action) and to give rise to transactions and propositions that can be accepted, negotiated, or rejected, have to attain a certain precision (an example of such a story might be: the wolf comes—he is nasty—the baby is afraid—Mother comes to help). Once accepted, the sequence of ideas constitutes the scenario or the development of the theme. Even among children at the early age of 3, a great variety of themes has been noted. Some are linked to real-life experience, called *realistic play* by Garvey (1982) (e.g., a birthday party, looking after a baby, a family outing); others are fantastic (superman, fairies, etc.) and are often based on stories told by adults or known from picture books or television. Even in realistic play, children do not simply reproduce known situations and events, but modify them and add ingredients of their own; in all pretend play, they combine, dissociate, and displace elements of experienced or observed events, whereas in fantastic play, the liberty to do so is much greater.

Sharing a Content.   Within the play, symbolizations have to be clearly indicated, and ideas and intentions made explicit if the fiction and the system of meanings are to be shared. Agreement, overt or tacit, is necessary and has to be maintained, often by way of compromise between conflicting intentions on the one hand and the desire to play together on the other, or between self-affirmation and submission. Agreement may be reached immediately or more gradually by reciprocal adjustments; it may be maintained without conflict (through clarification, confirmation, approbation, etc.) or negotiated after misunderstandings and disagreements.

Managing the Pretense.   The unfolding of the play has to be managed, especially when it becomes more complex. Management concerns the manner in which the action is carried out. As reported earlier (Verba, 1987a), the children elaborate form and content of the pretense simultaneously: They are not only playwrights and actors, but also stage managers. They give directives, comment on performances, create scenery. One child may take control during a whole episode, or several may take control in turn. When the partners are not of the same age, it is usually the oldest who takes charge (Verba, 1987b).

These diverse aspects of collective pretend play are also present in other collective activities (Verba, 1987a; Verba & Isambert, 1987), but symbolization confers on pretend play a specificity both on the content level and on the level of mutual comprehension, particularly when the play situation does not of itself suggest both theme and symbolic meanings (as is the case, e.g., when children play ''in the kitchen corner'').

Collective pretend play is usually studied in three different situations: free play without any objects, play with objects that evoke familiar social meanings (e.g., toy cups and plates, telephones, dolls), or play with familiar objects that do not evoke such meanings (e.g., building blocks). The setting and the objects available to the children influence the form, content, and unfolding of pretend play in many ways, precisely because they may or may not evoke the same meanings for the participants. If pretend play takes place in a setting that evokes an already known social situation (e.g., kitchen corner) it provides elements for play that are already shared by the partners. Consequently, their efforts to construct a pretend episode are mainly focused on the choice of a theme, on the coordination of the events to be enacted, the roles to be played, the expression of their feelings, and the nature of interpersonal relations. When no such setting serves as a play space, the children can no longer count on shared experiences evoked by the setting and have to construct—before or during the play activity—various symbolic meanings that are necessary for coherence. Similarly, when the children in their play use objects with conventional social meanings or when they adopt roles of well-known characters or of animals, the need to name them is much reduced. By contrast, when nonsocially defined objects are used, it is essential for their symbolic meaning to be made plain: A piece of wood can just as well represent a tree, as a man or a gun. The less the setting and the objects evoke already shared, socially determined events, the more the partners have to be explicit; but in all situations, the choice of a well-known theme facilitates the unfolding of the scenario, because it provides a frame of reference and an anchoring point.

Most authors consider verbal communication to play an essential part in the initiation and elaboration of pretend play. A distinction has been made (Fein, 1981; Garvey, 1982; Giffin, 1984) between utterances produced by the child as an actor playing a particular role—called *acting* or *in-frame communication* (e.g., a mother speaking to her baby, a physician talking to his patient)—and utterances produced as comments on the content, on the development, and on other elements of the fiction. These utterances, often called *metacommunicative* or *out-of-frame communication,* are necessary for choosing a theme, scenery or props, for distributing roles, evaluating the performance, and so on. The relative frequency of these two types of utterances during pretend play depends on the setting and the objects at the children's disposal, on the theme that has been agreed on, on the abilities of the participants as well as on their interpersonal relations and the experiences they already share.

Neutral settings, and objects that lend themselves to multiple use (for constructions and experiments as well as for pretend play) lead to frequent out-of-frame communications and are thus particularly suited for the study of the means by which young children succeed in constructing shared meanings. This type of situation was chosen for this chapter precisely in the interest of analyzing the processes by which 3-year-olds in the course of dyadic interaction elaborate a shared system of symbolic meanings that, when linked to a chosen theme, allow for the coherent development of a scenario.

THE OBSERVATIONS

Setting and Method

Children between the ages of 3 and 4 were observed while playing in their usual room in the day-care center. The objects at their disposal were blocks of several shapes and sizes, either solid or hollow; different sized beads; bits of cloth; wooden bars with holes; wheels; rods of various length; and a grid, a wooden plank, a solid triangle, an open triangle made of cardboard, a cardboard cylinder, and a wooden channel. These objects were familiar to the children and presented no particular interest or social meaning. They were placed on a low table, in no particular order, and the children were seated around the table. No specific instructions were given; the children were simply told that the objects were there for everybody and that they could do with them what they liked. The researcher, an adult already well-known to the children, video recorded their activities without intervening (except for the purpose of preventing accidents) but showing interest. Recording sessions lasted 30 minutes, or less if the group dispersed beforehand. The setting gave rise to many and varied activities, to exploration of the objects, to constructions as well as to symbolic activities. Only pretend-play episodes are reported here. Thirty-one episodes (of varied length and complexity) were extracted from the totality of the data as well as some episodes with only symbolizations. The continuity and coherence of the episodes is much more in evidence in the videotapes than in the write-ups given here.

Analysis of the Data

The principles of our analysis of the observational data have been described in earlier publications (Verba, 1982, 1985). They take into account the social and cognitive dynamics of the play episode in its totality and focus on the progression of the scenario and the processes by which shared meanings are established.

First, dyadic pretend-play episodes were extracted from the various collective activities. When such an episode was noted, its cognitive or social origin in the dynamics of the interaction was sought in order to determine the start of the episode. The end of the episode was determined simply by the dissolution of a partnership or by a clear change in the character of the play.

For each episode, all the behaviors of the partners (their actions on objects, their social exchanges, and their utterances) were transcribed. Each unit of analysis was either a pretend action or an interaction with the partner concerning that action. These units were subsequently categorized according to function: the establishment of socioaffective contacts, of shared symbolic meanings, of mutual understanding or agreement. One unit may have several functions: When a child addressing another who is playing alone says: *Will we play cars?*, the utterance attracts the other's attention, proposes an idea for play, and asks for the other's agreement. When the other responds with: *That's the car,* showing something he or she has constructed, the proposal is implicitly accepted, and a symbolic transformation is carried out on the object.

An overview of the episodes considered here is given before entering into a more detailed analysis of a number of protocols. Certain types of play and play themes as well as various functions of the children's utterances and distinct phases in the construction of the pretense can be distinguished.

Types and Themes of the Observed Episodes

In one type of episode, the children are mainly occupied with the attribution of symbolic meanings to objects, either to those that are at their disposal or to objects they have put together themselves. In the other type, the children construct a scenario with a theme and various pretend actions, which entail the symbolic transformation of objects, persons, and spaces, and a sequence of ideas and events. The themes developed in this second type are either inspired by the children's shared experiences of daily life, such as birthday parties, meals, washing up, looking after a baby or a sick child, or by stories and fairy tales they have been told; themes can also be fantastic products of free wheeling imagination. In rare instances, the theme can be a theatrical show, with some children as the audience and others as performers (e.g., when a child pretends to sing with a microphone, or manipulates an object as if it were a puppet).

Verbal Communication

In all the groups we observed there was much talking, both when the children were playing individually, and when they were engaged in collective play. In their interactions, the utterances serve various functions. As many authors have noted, children's talk serves to nourish the content of the pretend play by way of commenting on the symbolizations, the representation of events, the sequence of events, and so on. But children's utterances may also concern events and feelings that have nothing to do with the play (e.g., talk about an event that happened before they started to play, a boast about some accomplishment or possession, a comment about what is going on elsewhere in the room). Such deviations from pretend play are rare; when they do appear in the course of a dramatic episode, they may have the particular function of serving to decrease the psychological tension inherent in certain emotionally charged play situations (e.g., when some children were enacting a battle involving death and destruction, they abandoned the fiction at three different times and began to speak—calmly—about their shoes and about the weather). In general, comments on the pretense (metacommunication) were very frequent, but varied considerably from one episode to another.

Interactive Construction of a Scenario and its Phases

As noted by other authors, the construction of a pretend episode by children of our subjects' age or by older children (e. g., Forbes et al., 1986) goes through several distinct phases that may be described as the introduction of a theme, its development and, sometimes, its variation. In our observations, these phases may overlap or be combined; the age of the children, their personal relations, the time of the day, and many other factors play a part. A theme may be barely outlined, abandoned, and taken up again much later; at other times, an adopted theme may give rise to many ramifications that are but loosely linked to one another and to the theme. Often, however, the construction of a scenario shows a general pattern that may be described as follows.

Dyadic pretend play begins with the establishment of a contact between partners. The link between the two is often reaffirmed by positive socioemotional behavior. Once a partnership has been created, an action or a verbal proposal provides the impulse for a pretend episode. As the pretense develops, both partners contribute new ideas, adding to or combining with the initial proposal. Symbolic meanings are attributed to objects and actions, roles are distributed and pursued. If the proposals of one partner do not please the other, counterproposals are made and justifications are proffered in order to convince the partner and to reach agreement. Misunderstandings may arise, and are followed by explanations, clarifications, and arguments. It should be noted that a pretend episode does not always imply equal participation by each partner, neither as regards the creation of the scenario nor as regards its planning and management. Sometimes only one of the children functions as the creator of a scenario for as long as the other remains interested and collaborative. It should also be emphasized that it is rare for children as young as our subjects to propose a theme immediately except when they are used to playing together in the day-care center; generally they first play together in some other way, whereupon a pretend theme emerges in the course of their interaction.

As mentioned earlier, in one type of pretend episode the partners do not develop a theme, but are totally occupied with the attribution of symbolic meanings to various objects; in another type, these symbolic meanings will serve the unfolding of a scenario. Because our aim in this chapter is to analyze the establishment of such symbolic transformations of objects, we give examples of such sequences both when they occur in isolation, without further elaboration, and when they occur as steps toward a theme or during its elaboration.

THE ATTRIBUTION OF SYMBOLIC MEANINGS
TO OBJECTS IN ISOLATED SEQUENCES

In these sequences, the children name various meanings they give to objects without constructing a scenario or taking up roles, although sometimes they may perform some brief action with the objects. For the children, the interest of these particular sequences seems to lie in the symbolizations themselves, and in the exchanges they elicit. Symbolizations are communicated to the partner either by simple denomination or by utterances that may add further information; the objects are picked up and shown, and sometimes a pretend action is performed that reinforces the symbolic meaning as when a block is called an airplane and the child moves it in the air by hand.

The observations are given in full (leaving out very occasional nonrelated events) and the units of behavior are numbered vertically in their temporal order. For actions, facial expressions, and attitudes, ordinary characters are used; for the children's utterances, *italics*.

Example 1

[Translators' note: The children's speech in French (chapters 1 and 4) and Italian (chapters 2 and 3) differs from that of adults in those languages in ways that are not reproducible in English. Also with respect to vocabulary, it is difficult to render the exact flavor of what the children say. In a fairly literal translation, the children inevitably seem to have a better command of their language than they do in reality.]

Loic, 3;11   Barbara, 3;2

1) Puts a bead on a rod.
   Apple.

                                     2) Covers a small grid with a cloth.

3) *Give me the ball.*

                                     4) No answer.

5) Pushes rod plus bead into a cork.
   That's a light.

                                     6) Puts block on a cloth.
                                        Look at my sick child.

7) Constructs two other rods
   plus bead.
   That's a light.

                                     8) Adds another block.
                                        That's the sick child.

9) *I make light, that's also a sick child.*

10) *Where's the light?*
    Looks at L.

11) Puts a triangle onto a cube.
    It's the house.

12) Puts his lights around
    his house.
    Lights in the snow.

13) Puts a bead under the grid.
    That's the football.

14) Takes another bead,
    manipulates.
    That is also a football.

15) Takes the bead off the rod.
    That's the light.

In this example, both children in turn attribute symbolic meanings to the objects at their disposal or to combinations they have put together themselves. They attract one another's attention, name the objects, name them again, and look at one another. Loic gives three different symbolic meanings to his rod-plus-bead construction—apple, ball, light—and one to his cube-plus-triangle combination—house. Barbara gives a meaning to her block on a piece of cloth—a sick child—and to a bead—football. The children not only listen to one another, but take up one another's designations. Loic adopts Barbara's sick child, Barbara accepts Loic's light and asks where it is, and Barbara's football is adopted by Loic with reference to an identical bead. No pretend scenario follows these symbolic attributions: What interests the children are the symbolic transformations themselves, which are partly shared.

In some sequences, the reciprocal acceptance of various symbolic meanings attributed to the same object is total: Each partner proposes meanings that are immediately adopted by the other, as in the observation in Example 2.

Example 2

Marc, 4   Philippe, 3;6

1) Places a block in front of Philippe:
   Do you want another one?

2) *No, don't want it.*

3) *It's for fun this.*

4) Touches M.'s arm.

5) They look at one another and laugh.

6) Takes the bar with holes, shows it to Ph.: *That's a sting.*

[In French, *piqûre* is used for both a syringe and the injection, as well as for insect bites.]

7) No.

8) *There are two stings.* He looks at Ph. and shows him the other bar lying on the table. *There you have a sting.*

9) Looks, nods. *Yes, its a sting.* He takes an object, pretends to inject it with the bar and makes a noise.

10) *Yes, me too: that's the sting.* He pretends to inject, also with noise.

11) Holding the same bar: *That's a hammer.* He beats with it, then puts it down.

12) *Look, do you see my hammer?* He taps with it, observes M.

13) Asks M.: *Where is the hammer?*

14) *It's there.* Shows his bar to Ph.

[There ensues a brief exchange about their clothes.]

15) Observing M.: *Where's your gun?* He holds onto his bar.

16) *Well. . . my gun. . .* He looks at Ph. and roots among the objects.

17) *Your gun is there.* He points to the other bar on the table.

18) *My gun is there,* showing his original bar.

The same wooden bars become for both partners successively a syringe, a hammer, a gun. After an initial refusal by Philippe, Marc obtains Philippe's agreement by showing him that there is another wooden bar. The children name the objects, ask questions, look at one another, concur explicitly (*Yes, me too*), and perform symbolic actions according to the meaning given to the object (making piercing movements with the syringe, tapping with the hammer). After an initial disagreement, the two children play together more and more smoothly.

In other sequences, the children's interest in the attribution of symbolic meanings leads to the development of a pretend play theme however briefly, as in Example 3.

Example 3

Ludovic, 3;10

Aimel, 3;9

1) *Okay . . . there was one ball missing.* Places blue ball in front of A. and smiles.

2) *We're not going to put that one on. It'd fall.*

3) Holds the red ball on his nose: *That's a red nose.* Looks at A. and smiles.

4) She looks at L. Takes the blue ball. *That makes a big blue nose.*

5) Puts the red ball on his eye: *I have a biggy eye.* Looks at A.

6) Observes L. and waits.

7) Puts the red and the blue balls together: *That's us those little balls. We're them.*

8) Nods her head in agreement.

9) *Me I'm red.* Points to the red ball.

10) *And you're like that, OK?* Holds out the blue ball to A.

11) *No, you're like that, you're blue.* Looks at L.'s pullover.

12) *And I'm . . . red.*

13) He hides the red ball behind his neck. *I've got you.* Shows the red ball to A. and hides it again. *You're taken!*

[They smile at one another with eye contact.]

Ludovic proposes several symbolic meanings for the red and blue balls, which are accepted by his partner, who at one point proposes a small change and justifies it (the color of the balls should correspond to their pullovers). The balls first represent body parts (eye, nose), then the children themselves (*We are them*), and finally a distinction is made between "you" and "me," which allows for a differentiation of roles. Then Ludovic's idea of catching his partner (*I've got you*) and of hiding the red ball leads to a brief pretend game of hide-and-seek. The same processes of sharing symbolic meanings attributed to the objects are used in this observation as in the others: naming the objects, performing an action to make its symbolic function explicit (putting the little ball on one's nose or eye), taking up and sometimes enlarging one's partner's denomination (*That's a red nose—That makes a big blue nose*), proposing a change and justifying it.

Such sequences are frequent as an introduction to the adoption of a theme and its development. They also occur during a scenario as an ad hoc intermezzo serving as a link between different elements of the pretend sequence. The sharing of meanings is obtained by the strategies just outlined.

THE ATTRIBUTION OF SYMBOLIC MEANINGS IN PRETEND SCENARIOS

When the episode becomes more complex, symbolic meanings are attributed also to the actors, their actions, and the place and time of the pretend events. In these episodes, the children also communicate their personal meanings and reveal their intentions and wishes in order to obtain their partner's understanding and collaboration. Their task now is more difficult: They have to construct a common framework of reference in order to link the elements of the pretense in such a way that the theme can be developed coherently. The nature of the exchanges, that is, the fictional context of utterances and actions, the roles and the spatiotemporal situation of the scenario have to be made clear, and each partner has to adjust his or her ideas and wishes to those of the other. The analysis of such more complex episodes showed that, in general, the children indicate and explain every symbolic transformation that is introduced, either— as they feel it to be necessary—before, during, or immediately after a symbolic action. The sharing of meanings is facilitated whenever the pretend play incorporates a reference to shared social or institutional experiences, or to activities the children have already at some time carried out together. When the episode is based on individual experiences and is further removed from situations that are familiar to both partners, it becomes necessary to prepare the pretense and to interrupt it with indications, questions, justifications, corrections, and so on.

Three examples of such complex episodes are reported here in their totality;

although the extraction of certain parts would illustrate particular points, the coherence of the sequence as a whole would be obscured. The examples cover the range from a highly familiar theme (a family outing) to a scenario based on a fairy tale (*The Three Little Pigs*), which the children have heard but not necessarily understood in the same way, to a fantastic, almost surrealist scenario (death of a cannon).

Example 4

A Family Outing by Car

Here the two children use objects to which they had given symbolic meanings in an earlier episode: a triangular block for a car, and two big beads for mommy and daddy. The new episode is divided into two parts, of which the second takes up a suggestion made by one of the children in the first part.

Before they start, Aimel is busy making a construction of small blocks. Ludovic tries to attract her attention.

Ludovic, 3;10	Aimel, 3;9

1) *We'll play jump.*

      2) Continues with her blocks.

3) *Or it's the car, OK?*

Ludovic proposes two themes, and manages to capture Aimel's attention. She implicitly accepts the second theme and enters into the game by attributing to a small wooden triangle the symbolic meaning of a car.

      4) Puts a big red bead and a big blue bead into the triangle.

5) *Now we'll go, OK?*
Looks at A.

      6) Looks at L.

7) *Yesss!* (joyous emphasis)

      8) *We'll put in the doors.*
      She closes the top with another block.

Aimel gives shape to Ludovic's proposal: She creates the car and its occupants. Ludovic understands her meaning. The door, a new symbolic transformation, is explicitly named by Aimel (8). The two beads certainly represent people.

9) *No, because we do not yet have babies.*

10) Observes A.
Takes two little white beads, and
puts them in front of A.:
*Little balls, there are two babies who
are bored, I have two babies who are
bored.*

11) Is busy with the car.

12) Adjusts the door.
Wait. . .I. . .them (?). . .come later.
(Neutral voice)

13) Tries to place another block
against the opening. (Taking part
in A.'s construction)

14) *Why come later?*

15) *Because. . .*
She touches the blocks.

16) She adjusts the blocks.
There's the door.

17) Observes A. He smiles bending
his head down.

18) She pushes the car imitating its
noises.

19) *Here we are, we've arrived, everybody
out.*

20) *Why everybody out?*

The request for clarification (14) and the responses (15, 16) indicate that
both children see Aimel's actions as related to the theme. The children continue for a short while to drive the car; then A. sets about specifying the different roles to be played, and L.'s proposal about babies is elaborated. The theme
then changes into a conflict between parents and children.

Naughty Children

1) *Now the babies'll come.*

2) Observes A.

3) She takes the white beads and puts
them into the car.

4) *Ya ta ta tititi tata toto!*

Ludovic, who in a previous episode played the driver, objects to the idea that the babies drive the car:

5) *They going to drive?*
   (neutral slightly worried tone)

6) *We, we are a daddy and you're the mummy.*

7) She listens attentively.

After having reminded his partner of their respective roles, Ludovic takes up the pretend play again, and mimics that he is getting angry. From here on, Ludovic and Aimel's actions follow one another smoothly:

8) Looking into the car:
   Listen, we're getting angry!

9) She shifts the babies in the car.

10) In a stern voice: *We're all getting very angry!*

11) *Oh, look what they've done!*
    (Reproachful, in mother's role)

12) Looks at A, listens attentively.

13) *Daddy, Daddy!*
    (Baby's voice)

14) *He's driving Mummy's and Daddy's car.*
    (Father's voice)

15) *Moa, moa, bababo.*
    (Baby's babble), moves the car.

16) Gets up, menacing voice:
    I'm standing up, that's what.

17) *You just wait and see!*

18) Touches one of the babies:
    What are you doing in our car?
    (Reproachful in mother's role)

19) *Owah, nowah*
    (Whining, in baby's role).

20) Normal voice: *You're the daddy.*

As is often the case, some symbolic meanings are overtly attributed, but once the new theme is understood and accepted there follows a series of exchanges between the partners (6 to 16) where the children no longer feel the need to explain their intention because they already share a familiar social plan according to which they can organize and coordinate their utterances and actions. Once the theme is accepted, it would serve no purpose to step out of the pretend frame for additional clarification.

Example 5

The Three Little Pigs

Young children are often interested in pretend play based on stories they have been told or have seen on television. The collective construction of a coherent scenario then demands equal knowledge of characters and events that are themselves fictional. Because the children often have divergent and only partial knowledge of these matters, the coordination of their activities is difficult and calls for numerous explanations and specifications. The children who take part in playing the story of *The Three Little Pigs* have all heard it told in the day-care center, and thus dispose of a known framework. But the story deals with so many events, characters, and props that the partners are obliged to give many explanations. The episode reported here follows an episode played by the same two children on the same theme, but interrupted by an extraneous event. In the earlier episode, the children had already accepted the theme, constructed the house of the little pigs, and performed certain symbolic actions attributed to the wolf and to the pigs. The cause of the interruption was the destruction of the little pigs' house by another child. In the episode reported here, the theme is implicitly taken up again by one of the children and is introduced by his proposal to reconstruct the house.

Giao, 3;3   Séverin, 3;8

                                         1) *We'll make it again.*

2) Takes part in rebuilding the house.

                                         3) *There . . . the wolf . . . is in the chimney.*

4) *Oh the wolf . . .*

The invitation (1) to take up building the house again is understood by Giao. Séverin also indicates that the house has some connection with a wolf (3). Giao asks for more information.

5) *Is it us who are going to do the house?*
    He looks at S.

                                    6) Looks at G. *Yes.*
                                    He goes on building.

7) *Wait a moment.* He puts blocks into the house.

Now that the construction and the pretense have been explained (3, 6), the play can continue. Giao takes part by announcing his intention to play the wolf and takes up one of the blocks to represent the wolf.

8) Puts a block in front of the house.
The wolf. . .(Neutral voice)

9) *Let me in.* (Deep voice)

10) *No, the house is not yet ready.* (Neutral voice) He fixes the house.

11) *We'll put him. . . we'll put him in the fire at home.* (Neutral voice) He builds on his own.

12) Looks at G.'s building. *Oh, that's not pretty.*

13) *Not pretty.* (Confirming)

14) *Eh eh, Mama.* (Baby voice)

After some comments on the house, Séverin (14) picks up the pretense as the baby pig crying for help where Giao left off (9), but Giao is not sure how to go on.

15) *Who, who's going to come back?*

16) *It's the wolf!* (high voice)

17) *So that's it.*

18) He hands S. a bead and looks at him attentively.

19) *Hey, that's not the wolf!*

Disagreement about how the wolf is represented leads to an explanation by Séverin.

20) *That's how the wolf is.* Advancing with his fists on the table he imitates the wolf: *Poom, poom, poom.* (Deep voice)

21) *It's not ready.* Goes on building.

22) Sings and turns away.

With Séverin taking up building instead of pursuing the pretense, Giao apparently abandons the play, but is immediately called back by Séverin.

23) *Hey! You make the house of the little pigs.*

24) *You put that there!* Looks at G. for a long time.

25) *No no. He goes in the door.*

26) *He goes in the door, then the wolf can't get him.*

27) *You put it like that.* He puts in the door.

28) *No no, it's like that.*

29) *The wolf is inside, in the door with the key there.* Points to a block and looks at S.

30) Points to a part of the building. *That's the door with the lock.*

The discussion is inconclusive and S. now proceeds to a general explanation:

31) *That's also the door with a lock.* Points to a different block.

32) Observes intensively.

33) *That's the ceiling.*

34) *The chimney there.*

35) Takes up a block. *A little pig who wants to come in.*

36) Takes a block and puts it in the building: *Another one there.*

In the course of these exchanges, the partners negotiated the function of the door (26, 29) and several other meanings (31-36) that will facilitate reproducing the story. The two children went on with the story without, however, reaching total coordination.

In this example, three in-frame acts (9, 14, 16) require 32 metacommunications for the children to share symbolic meanings and to construct the setting. The children explain their intention either spontaneously or following a question from their partner. There is some opposition between the two, they have disagreements and misunderstandings leading to efforts at adjustment by rectification and argument. There are also implicit references to known elements of the story, which are sometimes perfectly understood: when Séverin says *Let's make it again* (1), Giao immediately starts to construct "it" (i.e., the little pigs' house). Similarly, Séverin's premature reference to the wolf is accepted without question by Giao (3, 4). But difficulties arise; there are several problems concerning the door and the chimney of the house (26–33). In this episode, the children did not manage to construct a total scenario, despite the coherence of certain parts; at our subjects' age, such complex stories do not yet appear as lengthy, well-constructed pretend sequences.

Example 6

Death of a Cannon

The construction of fantastic scenarios is beset with difficulties for young children. Because fantasies are personal regarding both their elements and their temporal development, the partners may easily lapse into separate monologues, joining again from time to time only, and often more or less by chance. In Example 6, the children share many symbolic meanings, and construct some coherent sequences, but inconsistencies and difficulties in coordination persist. The theme is mainly developed by one of the children in a sequence of ideas that his partner tries to understand and does succeed in elaborating from time to time.

This episode followed a play sequence in which a cannon, a combination of three objects, was made to attack two children. There ensued a three-sided battle. After this short interlude, the cannon was placed on the table. The play was soon taken up again, but this time by only two children and along increasingly unusual lines.

Mikaël, 3;11   Julie, 2;9

1) Takes a small car out of his pocket
   and imitates noise of a siren:
   Wheeee!

                                                          2) Turns and looks at M.

3) Repeats the siren.

Having attracted Julie's attention, Mikaël needs to give some explanations for the action to continue.

4) *It's for the police.*

5) *Hooeee!*

6) *I made wheee for the police, they put out their lights.*

7) She observes M.

8) Together they imitate the siren, crescendo.

9) Takes an object out of his pocket. *There's another policeman coming up.*

10) Listens attentively.

11) Takes the cannon and sweeps the table as his field of fire.

12) *You saw it. I smashed everything.*

13) *And I'm going to kill him with that.* She attacks the cannon with a cube.

14) *The cannon is coming!*

15) She watches M.

16) *The police is going to attack the cannon.* (Emphatically)

17) *He's dead.* (Neutral voice)

Each pretend action is announced or commented on for the benefit of the partner. But Mikaël's last utterance is not sufficiently explicit about who is dead. The idea of killing the cannon is taken up again by Julie, and Mikaël's reiteration creates an area of agreement between them.

18) Observes J. and holds the cannon.

19) She holds a stick representing a person: *He's going to attack the cannon.* (Neutral voice)

20) *Boommm! Boom!* She hits the cannon with the stick.

21) *The cannon is dead, the cannon is dead. . .* (Emphatically)

22) Watches and listens.

23) *We're going to stick the cannon in the garbage can.* (Neutral tone)

24) *I saw him.* He points to a block. *He's wounded.* (Narrative tone, out of frame)

25) *OK... but him.* She points to another block. *He's not wounded.*

26) *Sure not. He didn't do anything.*

27) Imitates a siren, *You saw that one.* Points to an object. *He's going to call the police.*

28) *Why?*

29) *Because...*

30) *There's the police now. You saw it?*

31) Listens attentively.

32) *What's going on?* (High voice, in frame)

33) She continues to watch M.

34) *He's sick.* Points to an object and groans. (In frame)

35) Shoves an object and imitates the noise of a car.

36) *He's... going...?*

37) *Yes he's going to go out.*

38) Points to an object. *Oghm! Are they going to kill him?*

39) *Isht, isht* (battle noise). He points the cannon towards the sky. *Isht, isht.*

40) Takes a stick and fences with the cannon.

41) *He's dead.* (Neutral voice)

42) *Sure is.*

43) *OK, we'll put him in the hole afterwards.* She turns towards the adult.

44) *Yes, we'll stick him in the garbage.* He throws down the cannon.

45) *Yes, and then we'll put him in the cellar.*

In this, like in the preceding observation, many utterances deal with comments on the scenario, with explanations, clarifications, and so on. Particular to this episode is the fact that the children do not themselves act as persons or animals taking part in the scenario, but attribute these roles to objects and then proceed to describe them and to comment on their actions. It seems to be easier for these children to impersonate the characters by objects and to tell a story about them than to play the roles themselves. The number of characters and props as well as the lack of a familiar sequence make it difficult for the partners to work together and to share each other's thoughts.

As we supposed from the start, the sharing of a system of meanings is a precondition for the development of a coherent pretend-play sequence. The following final example in this chapter further illustrates the difficulties encountered by partners who lack a familiar framework: Confusion reigns and the partners disperse.

Example 7

Dead-End Dialogue

This episode followed the three-sided battle with the cannon and preceded by a few minutes the "death of a cannon" recounted in Example 6 with the same two children taking part. An unexplained element is introduced, which creates confusion.

Mikaël	Julie
1) Points the cannon to the sky. *Bang bang bang!* [*Peuf!* in French]	
	2) Holds a stick and looks at M. *That's going to make a fire.*
3) *You have fire on the oil.* Points to the stick and looks at J.	
	4) Looks at M.: *Where, where, where?*
	5) She looks at the objects on the table. *The blue one?* [N.B. French *feu* (fire) rhymes with *bleu* (blue)]
6) *The blue? Where's the blue one?*	
	7) Turns to another child: *Give the blue one.*

8) The two partners look all over the table. They seem confused and the play is given up.

In this example, the children do not understand one another's intentions, although they do interact, look at one another and ask questions. There is no shared social knowledge to help them. Curiously there seems to be a phonetic thread linking their utterances, which are not clarified despite the questions. Mikaël's *peuf* seems to lead to Julie's *feu*, which in turn seems to lead to *bleu*. In contrast with Examples 4 and 5, where the children had a common base of knowledge, although the base differed—real life as against story—Example 6 shows the effect of the absence of such a base. In Example 7, the lack of mutual comprehension remains total with cessation of play as a result.

CONCLUDING REMARKS

Interindividual coordinations in pretend play demand a sharing of the personal meanings that arise from each child's own experience and imagination. The coherence of a scenario depends on their ability to construct a common framework of meanings attributed to objects, actions, persons, and events. The setting and the available objects evoke, in greater or lesser degree, an organizing framework that facilitates a coherent development of a pretend sequence. In our observations, the objects the children had at their disposal and the absence of any instructions or incitations given by an adult left them free to go in for a variety of activities, often suggested by the physical properties of the objects; but they also pursued pretend activities in which the nature of the objects played no part. In the pretend episodes, the objects were simply used as a support for the children's creative imagination. The nonsuggestive character of the objects led to a wide variety of themes, ranging from the realistic to the fantastic. Two aspects of our observations are discussed in the following.

The Construction of Pretend-Play Episodes

All the pretend episodes show the establishment of socioaffective relations, the children's creative abilities, and their management of pretend play. The socioaffective aspect is especially clear at the start of an episode, when the partners establish contact and manifest their desire to play together; but it also contributes to maintaining the play when difficulties arise, difficulties that might lead to play breaking down. Looking at one another, smiling, laughing, and so on reinforce the emotional fusion between partners.

Out-of-frame communication (i.e., talk and, rarely, gestures or actions about the play) is essential for interactive organization and proved to be frequent in our observations. The children comment on their play amplifying its content, and sometimes introduce narratives that, although having a link with the pretend sequence, interrupt its dynamic development. It was not always easy to decide whether a particular utterance was *about* the pretense or *within* the pretense. When a child having taken the part of the father who supervises his children says to his partner: *We're getting angry!* (Example 4) is he speaking to his partner in his role as the father or is he telling her about the next phase of the scenario? Certain indications may make it possible to decide. When the children remain within the pretend frame, they often speak with special intonation, trying to imitate the voice of the character they are representing. They also speak with special emphasis, they gesture, mimic, and act while speaking. When they speak *about* the scenario, they explain, ask questions, give instructions, and so forth, in their normal voice and cease to act. On this point, our observations correspond to those of other authors including Giffin (1984) and Orsolini (1986).

Overall, metacommunicative units are twice as frequent in our observations as within-frame units. Between the various episodes, however, there are considerable differences: Sometimes the proportion of out-of-frame communications is much higher (e.g., 32 out-of-frame as against 3 in-frame communications in the example of *The Three Little Pigs*). By contrast, in the example of the family outing, 10 pretend units follow one another without interruption. In some episodes, the children's interest in the pretense gives way almost totally to their interest in the construction of a scenario and in the ensuing negotiations and discussions. Our analysis of the communicative units in the episodes showed a surprising number of actions and utterances that were meant to ensure reciprocal comprehension. For the children who produce these communications, they are doubly important: They clarify the child's own thoughts so that the partner's collaboration is facilitated, and they make it possible to eliminate disagreements by negotiation and to convince the partner of the value of a proposal. Such negotiations during play episodes that are not subject to preestablished conventional rules constitute, in our view, an equilibrium or a compromise between self-affirmation and the desire to maintain collaboration. The children argue for their own point of view, or modify it in the face of what the other child suggests, or even give up their own idea entirely, either because they become convinced or because they are complaisant. Negotiations are a complex socioaffective–cognitive mode of functioning, into which enter social influences and personal motivations not within the scope of this chapter.

Sharing of Meanings

All the observed episodes incorporate symbolic transformations that have to be shared for pretend play to develop. The most frequent transformations are those of objects. In all the episodes without exception, object transformation occurs, although at times only momentarily and for one partner only. In general, however, transformations are part of sustained interactions. They may make up a play sequence by themselves, as in our first two examples, and are often accompanied by actions to illustrate or clarify the symbolic meaning (e.g., tapping with an object named a hammer). Such sequences have, to our knowledge, not been reported previously, although they are clearly linked to genuine pretend play and often serve for initiation or continuation. They are evidence of the children's desire to pretend together and to use their capacities for imaginative representation. Naming the chosen representative of the object is the usual way of informing the partner of its symbolic meaning, sometimes supplemented by further clarification and information, either given verbally or through some action with the object. The next chapter includes a long sequence of exchanges concerning the functioning of what is meant to represent the siren of a ship. These various means of getting one's partner to share one's ideas can be used simultaneously (an utterance accompanied by an action or gesture) or successively, serving both an explanatory aim and the entry into the world of pretense. They may be accompanied by utterances that serve to maintain the partner's interest (*there you are, look, here it is*). Some children use subtle means to get their partner to accept proposals for personal symbolic meanings.

In general, the analysis of the pretend episodes shows that attributing meaning to ''neutral'' objects creates an empathic and collaborative atmosphere favorable to the construction of a scenario. Interestingly, the same object may be used to signify several objects or persons as in Example 1 where a rod with a bead represents successively an apple, a light, and a sick person; the sick person is represented by a block, a different block and a second rod-plus-bead assembly. These rapid changes in symbolic meaning indicate the mobility of the children's representative abilities, and reflect at a higher cognitive level the quick succession of actions on objects at the sensorimotor period. At our subjects' age, the range of possible representations is extended and increasingly detached from material reality.

When the attribution of symbolic meanings to objects is used in the construction and development of a pretend theme, these symbolizations appear either at a particular moment of the scenario in order to provide a needed prop, or form part of an extended series of exchanges between the partners. In Examples 3 and 4 they serve the inauguration of a theme, and in Examples 5 and 6 they function as clarifications or as reminders of the theme. The same means of sharing the various symbolic transformations of objects are used in all situations.

Other transformations concern the roles the partner are going to play in the general context of the pretense. Roles may be announced explicitly before the scenario starts or before a new phase is introduced, as in Example 5: daddy and mommy, or by allusion as in Example 6: *the wolf. . .* said in a neutral voice, followed by *let me in* said emphatically in a deep voice. When the pretend play is based on shared knowledge and some objects have already acquired shared symbolic meanings, the children may directly assume a role (as was done in Example 6 by the child who called for mommy in a baby voice). Short allusions, special intonations, and symbolic actions often help the partner to play a role more convincingly.

A major difficulty for children of our subjects' age arises when each partner has to play different roles in more complex scenarios that demand interactions between several persons and animals, as was already reported by Garvey and Berndt (1977). In the excitement of the children's play, shifts may occur that necessitate clarifications and reminders. In the second part of Example 4, Aimel first plays the part of the mother, then that of a baby; when Ludovic, who plays the father, also pretends to be a baby, Aimel reminds him of his role. Episodes such as that of *The Three Little Pigs* are even more difficult because each of the two partners has to assume several roles: the wolf, the mother pig, and a baby pig. Moreover, their acting has to be coordinated within a story frame that is not entirely shared by the partners, in contrast with scenarios based on familiar events. Although the children make great efforts to signal the part they play to their partner, misunderstandings occur and the management of the theme's development, because it is not clearly foreseen, can only be carried out step by step. Cognitive problems other than the sharing of meanings arise during efforts to coordinate roles. It is hardly surprising that at our subjects' age this coordination remains tentative and is sometimes not achieved at all.

The distribution of roles is in general very supple. Regarding persons, no boy ever played the part of a mother, nor a girl the part of a father. But for nonsexually typed roles each partner may play several and it even happens that both partners play the same part, sometimes quasi-simultaneously, in different phases of the scenario (in Example 5, both children at different times play the wolf as well as a baby pig). This multiplicity of parts appears to contribute to the children's growing awareness of the existence of different points of view: The relations between signifiers and signifieds become varied and changeable, and favor a decentration from the child's own point of view, a comparison with somebody else's point of view, and eventually a coordination between the two. The importance of such decentration and coordination for the construction of mental operations is well established.

The children use a variety of means to communicate their intention of entering the sphere of pretend action. In our observations, with the objects at the children's disposal, the possibilities for shared activities are numerous, and any shift away from material action on the objects toward pretend play needs to be made clear. Sometimes a theme is proposed forthwith, but this is rare at our subjects' ages, except in the case of well-known themes or when an already shared episode is taken up again. More often, the theme is progressively constructed, as reported by other authors also. The proposal to initiate a pretend play is often signaled by a symbolic action or the attribution of a symbolic meaning to an object, either explicitly and verbally (e.g., in Example 5: *That's the door,* or Example 4: *Now the babies'll come*) or implicitly by successive allusions. Occasionally, one child may remind the other of the pretend frame, and a shift toward real activities may also be signaled.

Although most of our observed episodes are clearly interactive, moments of individual activity occur; but usually the children come together again, either by an act of imitation or by a return to an already shared frame of symbolic meanings. The children are clearly aware of the necessity to communicate the meanings they attribute to the objects, to actions and to the situation in general; during their exchanges they progressively create a common space of thinking, determined by the clarification of their intentions and their comments on the meaning of their symbolic transformations. By reference to this space, each partner can introduce new elements for the other to assimilate; both can thus understand the fictive character of utterances and actions. Their comprehension is also shown in various ways: either explicitly, by saying *yes* or *right*, or implicitly by performing an action that is appropriate to the proposal, or by smiling, nodding, and so on. Each element of the system activates other meanings that need not be expressed. As the shared space grows, nourished by the experience of the interaction of the moment as well as by other social and interindividual experiences, the play becomes increasingly collaborative and the various activities combine in a coherent scenario.

In certain scenarios we observed what we called *confrontations*. Taken in a general sense, this means that the children in turn express different proposals and that they compare their own intentions with those of their partner. Such confrontations lead to negotiations and discussions, and allow the observer to apprehend the processes of reciprocal adjustment. It appears that, already at age 3, children may use authoritarian strategies, but that more often they try to interest their partner in their proposals and show that they are ready to follow the other's ideas and to modify their own.

Regarding the more general question of the possible contribution made by collective pretend play to cognitive and communicative development, the sharing of symbolic meanings may be supposed to consolidate certain types of knowledge. On the one hand, as we have seen, shared meanings form networks that facilitate social interaction among peers and favor collaboration in various activities. On the other, the means adopted by the children to establish a shared-meaning system—confrontation and negotiation as well as transmission of information and guiding—lead to the beginnings of a certain organization of social interaction that will remain important throughout life and that will contribute to the objectivation and acquisition of knowledge. These basic interactive processes can be used by educators (e.g., Pontecorvo, 1987). Very similar processes are also at work in other collective activities, and at other ages, as shown in several observational studies (e.g., Verba, 1987a).

In our view, the study of collective pretend play among young children clarifies the origins of "equilibrated exchanges of thought" considered by Piaget to be necessary for the elaboration of all knowledge. In collective pretend play, the ability to construct a common framework of reference, to conserve proposals, and to maintain relations of reciprocity is clearly already present before the age of 4.

ACKNOWLEDGMENTS

I am grateful to the children of the Max Jacob Day-Care Center in Paris for their inventive play and to the staff of the center for their valuable collaboration.

Chapter 2

Pretend Play in the Schoolyard: Propagation of Play Themes Among a Group of Young Children*

Tullia Musatti
Susanna Mayer
*Consiglio Nazionale
delle Ricerche, Roma*

Many studies have shown that the setting in which collective play among young children takes place influences the type of play, its themes, and its development. Despite Darvill's (1982) admonition to take into account, or at least to be aware of, the multiple features of the environment in which a play sequence is observed, there are still very few studies where an effort has been made to relate certain particularities of the environment to characteristics of play.

Observations of children's play in the schoolyard have generally led to analyses of social interaction among children. It is true that, when children are away from the classrooms of the day-care center or the kindergarten and playing in the much larger space of the yard, aspects of their interactions can be observed that are not seen at home, in the center, in the schoolroom, or in the laboratory. Play in the yard has also led to studies of the development of friendship between two or more children, showing the stability of such relationships despite the fluidity of the children's choice of partners for play. In addition, several authors (e.g., Moore & Young, 1979; Osorina, 1986) studied the various ways children formed groups in the playground and observed that these were always characterized by the creation of a separation from the adults present, in contrast with the frequently noted tendency of children to cluster around the adult in other locations.

In this chapter, our analyses of pretend play among 3-year-olds in the yard focus on two of its aspects that are linked to features of this location: absence

---

*This chapter is based on observations made in a day-care center in Rome.

of a setting organized by adults (i.e., no toys, books, dolls, etc.) and spaciousness (leading to much moving about and fluid groups).

It was already observed (Musatti, 1983) that, even at the age of 2, children are capable of constructing long play sequences together when they have objects at their disposal whose social use they are familiar with. We also observed that they sometimes attributed unexpected meanings to these objects, without creating difficulties of comprehension (Musatti & Mayer, 1987). It might be supposed that, in the absence of objects to suggest themes for pretend play, few such episodes would occur and that the presence of swings, slides, and so on, would direct the children mainly toward other types of play. Surprisingly, this was not the case: Many pretend-play episodes were observed. We consequently endeavored to analyze by what means the children managed to construct coherent sequences around a theme with various symbolic meanings in this setting, despite fluid groups and frequent displacements. We supposed that, if there were pretend-play episodes, they would be enacted by two or three children who might get together for a short time in relation to a theme and that the play would come to an end when they dispersed. Our very first observations showed that contrary to expectation, symbolic meanings are propagated and play themes are developed over time as well as over space.

In this chapter, we intend to discuss, on the one hand, the understanding and transmission of symbolic meanings and themes and, on the other, the mechanisms of their propagation and development at different times, in different locations, and among different groups.

THE OBSERVATIONS

Setting and Methods

The yard of the day-care center in which the observations were made is L-shaped running along two sides of the building for a width of about 10 meters (33 feet) and a total length of about 120 meters (400 feet). The surface is grass with a narrow sidewalk adjacent to the building. There is a space with a swing for several children, one with a merry-go-round, and one with a slide. Few movable objects are permanently present in the yard: some buckets and spades, a few bowling pins, and several small plastic boats. Sometimes the children bring toys into the yard (e.g., dolls). The yard itself furnishes grass, weeds, pebbles, sand, and so on, to play with. During spring and summer, between 30 and 45 children play there without the staff proposing any special activities. From the numerous videotapes made in this setting, 20 collective pretend-play episodes (of between 5 and 45 minutes duration) comprising one or several connected themes were selected for full transcription and for various types of analyses (interactions between the children and how they are regulated, strategies of explanation and demonstration, choice of spatiotemporal contexts, etc.). For this chapter, three examples illustrate the ways in which pretend themes are socialized between children when they play in the yard.

Example 1 concerns the transmission of one particular theme, first from one child to his partner, and then to some other children who join in; then the first partner transmits the theme to a third child who in turn shares it with a fourth. The symbolic meaning of the object that supports their pretense remains unchanged. The sequence thus illustrates the propagation of a single theme.

Example 2 shows how different meanings are attributed to one object, the acceptance or refusal of other children to whom it is proposed, and how the different meanings attributed to an object lead to the symbolic transformation of a particular area in the yard.

The third example illustrates the complexity of propagating an initial theme that comprises numerous symbolic objects and activities, and that is enacted at different times in different areas. In a way, this last example combines the two aspects illustrated separately in the two previous ones.

Example 1

The Siren of the Boat

Eight children are seated on the sidewalk, playing with small plastic boats (blocks of monochrome plastic having the outline of a ship with masts imprinted in relief).

1) Lorenzo (3;1) has a boat in his hand, and says to Marco (3;0): *Let's try!* He turns toward the adult observer, smiles, presses with his thumb on the foremast and says *Beee . . . beee . . . beee.* Marco, who holds an identical boat in his hand, observes Lorenzo attentively and also says *Beee . . . beee . . . beee.* He then also turns to the adult, still holding the boat simply in his hand, and the two children say together: *Beee . . . beee . . . beee!* They then look at one another and smile.

2) Lorenzo once again says: *Beee . . . beee . . . beee!* pushing with his thumb on the mast as before, while Marco repeats the sounds without pushing on the mast.

3) Lorenzo bends down, points to Marco's hands and then to the fore of Marco's boat, saying: *Look, there you can make the sound!* Marco again says his *beees* without pressing on the mast, but looking successively at Lorenzo's boat and at Lorenzo himself.

4) When Marco once again simply utters the sounds, Lorenzo points to the boat and says softly: *There!* Marco, however, continues as before looking at Lorenzo, at Lorenzo's boat, and then at his own boat, saying once again: *Beee . . . beee . . . beee.*

5) Lorenzo then again presses on the mast and produces the sounds. Finally, Marco begins to press with his two thumbs on both the masts of his boat, saying: *Beee . . . beee . . . beee!* Andrea (3;2) who has been attentively observing the two boys then also begins to emit the sounds, while lifting up his own boat and showing it to a fourth child.

6) Lorenzo and Marco look at one another, smiling with satisfaction, and continue to produce the sounds and to push on the masts of their boats. Lorenzo, like Marco, now pushes on both masts. Andrea is momentarily distracted by another child.

7) Lorenzo gets up and walks a few steps away, followed by Marco and Andrea; he then turns toward the adult and repeats the sounds while pushing with his thumbs: Marco also turns, looks at Lorenzo, and does the same. After a short interruption, Lorenzo turns to Andrea, once again performing the same actions and producing the sounds. Andrea looks at him attentively, simply produces the sounds at first and then puts his hands in the correct position on the boat. All three children begin to run around the yard, crying: *Beee . . . beee . . . beee!* holding the boats at chest height and pushing on the masts. Several other children look at them.

In this example, the pretense is a simple one and consists of two actions, carried out simultaneously: pressing on the masts and uttering a sound. In the way Lorenzo does it, pressing the mast seems to cause the sound, and this is apparently not immediately understood by the other children.

When Lorenzo first proposes his idea of playing in a certain way with the boats (i.e., to pretend that their sirens are sounding), Marco agrees immediately (1), but does not take up the pressing action. Lorenzo tries to correct Marco, and shows him how to do it properly (3 and 4). When Marco understands and uses both thumbs to press on both masts (5), Lorenzo takes up the two-mast idea (6). Andrea joins in the play (5), and all three children start running around joyfully (7), attracting the attention of several others. Cries of *Beee . . . beee . . . beee* and laughter can be heard all around the yard. About 10 minutes after the exchanges between Lorenzo, Marco, and Andrea, Marco stops running next to a group of little girls who are sitting in a semicircle busily tearing leaves into small bits, which they put into plastic buckets. Marco still has his boat in his hand.

8) Marco approaches Noemi (3;1), one of the girls in the group, and says: *And for me?* Noemi points to the boat and answers: *You give me that then.* The two children quickly and smoothly exchange boat for bucket, and are observed by Francesca (2;11), who is sitting next to Noemi.

9) As soon as Noemi has the boat in her hand, Marco points to the mast and says: *Press on that button, OK!* Noemi looks bewildered, but Marco insists:

That's where you press. Wait . . . there! and points to the mast again. After an exchange of complicitous smiles, Marco is busy with his bucket and Noemi starts to push with one finger alternately on each of the two masts. She then rather hesitantly turns the boat around in her hands.

10) Marco says something to Noemi who answers (neither utterance could be interpreted). Noemi, holding the boat up in the air, shows it to Francesca.

11) Marco says to Noemi: *Don't take it away with you, eh!* Noemi shakes her head, presses on the forward part of the boat, holds the boat out to Marco, and asks him a question (inaudible). Marco takes the boat, puts it on the ground and presses with his forefinger on the foremast; he then turns to Noemi, hands the boat back to her, saying: *There you are!* and while still pressing on the mast: *This one here!* Noemi takes the boat and turns it in her hands, touching the masts at different points.

12) Noemi turns to Francesca and shows her the boat; she takes Francesca by the wrist and makes her press with her open hand on the boat, then, saying: *No, like this!* she makes Francesca press with one finger on one of the masts. Francesca starts pressing on her own, while Noemi holds the boat for her. The two girls smile at one another.

13) Noemi turns toward Marco and offers him the boat. Marco takes it, pushes with his two thumbs on the two masts, and (at last!) introduces the *Beee . . .* sound, saying it softly before giving the boat back to Noemi, who, after a short pause, presses on the foremast and also says: *Beee . . .* softly. Marco looks at her, nods with a serious expression on his face, and says: *Yes!*

14) After the children have been distracted for a moment by some other children playing at a distance, Noemi again presses the fore part with her thumb and asks, showing the boat to Marco: *Here?* Marco takes the boat while Noemi still has her hand on it, looks at it seriously and answers: *Yes!* But Noemi changes the position of her hands, Marco takes it from her and says: *No no, not there! You don't press there, you press here!* indicating the fore part. Noemi takes the boat once more and presses with her two thumbs on the forward part; Marco approves: *Right, that's where you press.* Noemi continues to press and says softly: *Beee . . .* Marco nods and says: *Yes.*

15) Noemi once again shows Marco the boat, and pointing to the forward part asks: *Is that where you press?* Marco looks, nods affirmatively, but is busy putting bits of leaves into his bucket. Noemi insists and takes Marco by the arm in order to make him touch the boat again. Marco presses once again and says: *Beee . . .* Noemi, finally satisfied, smiles, presses the same spot as Marco several times saying: *Beee. . .*

16) Marco takes the boat back, gently but firmly, gets up and walks away; Noemi takes up her bucket.

The second part of this episode starts and ends with an exchange of objects.

As before, the theme centers on a boat and the way it should be handled to make its siren work. Marco explains to Noemi, and Noemi explains to Francesca exactly where to press (9, 11, 12). Marco seems to base his explanations on the point that he himself had difficulty in grasping when Lorenzo made his demonstrations; the production of the sound was never a problem. Maybe this is the reason why Marco only later (13) produces a soft *Beee...* Noemi also seems to attach great importance to the right spot to press, and asks several times for reassurance. Both children act as if there were a real causal link between the spot to press and the production of sound, instead of a fictional link created by Lorenzo: They are as meticulous in their ways of pressing the masts as if indeed it were only this precise action that could produce the sound. Because the pretend theme is that of a boat with a working siren, the action of making the sound would seem to be the most important part of the play. Paradoxically, transmitted from one child to another and then to a third, the sound production is almost forgotten. In other episodes as well, such meticulosity in reproducing certain actions was noted; it seems that the message "do as I do" can easily become "this is the way it should be done," especially when the pretense comprises a complex notion of causality, which for young children is still steeped in magicophenomenist thinking.

Example 2

Gun or Oar?

Two successive transformations of an object are proposed by one child. Others join the game.

Example 2.1

That's a Gun

1) Alessio (2;7) has found two fat plastic bowling pins and is walking with them in the garden. He stops and, holding the two pins again his eyes, says: *Pim, pim, pim, pam.* He goes on walking holding the pins as before: *Pam!* It is obvious to the observer that he is pretending to aim and shoot with a gun. Next he approaches Laila (2;0) who is trying to ride a bicycle.

2) Alessio points the pins at the girl and cries *Paaam!* Laila looks at him attentively, then takes up her pedaling again, and says to him: *No pam!* She turns away.

3) Alessio then goes on walking and keeping the pins up against his eyes. He approaches the swing on which Lucia (2;3) and Elisabetta (2;8) are sitting, one facing the other. Lucia looks at the bowling pins and says to Alessio: *Give me one* pointing to the pin Alessio is holding in his right hand. Then she adds:

That one. Alessio replies: *Not that one; that one* referring to the other pin.

The negotiation between the two children continues with Lucia insisting and Alessio refusing. After a while the discussion dies down.

4) Alessio now turns to Elisabetta and, pointing at her with one of the pins, says: *Turn around, turn!* Elisabetta does not reply. Alessio next addresses Lucia saying: *Turn . . . you turn around also!* and then: *But are you crazy, are you crazy?* Lucia does not react. After a while Alessio gives up and walks off saying: *I'm going to shoot with two guns.*

5) A little later, Alessio returns with two other bowling pins and gives them to Lucia and to Elisabetta. Lucia says to him: *Give it,* by way of acceptance. During these exchanges, another girl, Angela (3;0) joins the group. She asks Alessio: *And for me?* Alessio answers: *I'm going to get other guns for you* and runs off.

Angela after a while says softly: *Alessio, guns, Alessio.*

6) Alessio returns with four bowling pins and says: *Two guns, one for me and one for you.* Angela holds out her hand to take the bowling pins: *Give!* Alessio gives her two bowling pins and emphatically points out: *Two, see.* Angela adds: *Just like . . . just like you.*

In the meantime, Lucia and Elisabetta continue to hold their bowling pins without saying a word.

7) Alessio says to Angela: *Are we going to shoot?* Angela points to the single pin kept by Elisabetta: *She's got one* and to the pin kept by Lucia: *Also one.* Alessio, taking up the commentary from when the theme started, says: *And we've got two.*

8) Angela puts her two pins to her chest and shouts: *Doo.. doo.. ba.. ba.. ba.. ba..!* She turns to look at Alessio, no doubt seeking approval, but Alessio corrects her: *No, you put them here* and he slowly lifts the bowling pins to his eyes. Angela comes back with an *Eh?* and Alessio repeats: *You put them here.* Angela tries to hold the pins the way Alessio does, then removes one of the pins from her eye to check on Alessio and tries again, remaining motionless with the pins pressed to her eyes. Alessio also removes one of his pins to check on Angela and is not satisfied: *No, not like that, like this!* Angela, keeping the pins before her eyes asks: *Like this?* but Alessio insists: *No, no, like this.* Angela again removes one of the pins the better to watch Alessio, who, now satisfied, puts the pins in front of his eyes and cries: *Pa, pa, pa.* Angela imitates him at once.

The two children move a few steps away from the swing and go on pretending to shoot for quite a while. Lucia and Elisabetta, who are still sitting on the swing, watch it all attentively.

9) Alessio approaches the swing and addresses Lucia and Elisabetta: *You are not shooting.* Angela intervenes and encourages Elisabetta: *Go on, shoot!* to which Elisabetta replies: *I don't shoot.*

Alessio now turns to Lucia: *And you, you don't shoot?* Lucia replies with a decisive: *No!*

Angela puts her bowling pins down, snatches Elisabetta's pin and tries to hold it against one of Elisabetta's eyes, but Elisabetta turns her head away. Angela tries again. *Aoh!* But Elisabetta refuses, shaking her head and covering her eyes with her arms.

10) Alessio then says to Angela: *So it's us who are going to shoot, just us.* Angela proposes: *Both of them.* She points to the two other little girls and repeats: *Both of them.* Alessio, who is already lifting the bowling pins back into position, exclaims *It's us who are shooting!* Turning his back to the swing he proceeds to shoot.

Angela also starts shooting, but aims at the two other girls. For a while the shooting continues.

11) Alessio approaches Lucia for yet another try: *The two of you . . .* Disdainfully Lucia and Elisabetta leave the swing and move off. Alessio is angry and mutters: *Look at those creeps, nasty creeps!* and Angela echoes: *Nass . . . nasty creeps.*

In this observation, the theme—shooting with guns—is as simple as in Example 1: An object is symbolically transformed, the bowling pin becomes a gun, and is handled in a given way with accompanying imitative sound. The theme is created by Alessio (1) who proposes it successively to several children. His first attempt is with Leila (2) but she flatly refuses to play (*No Pam!*). He tries again with two other girls, Lucia and Elisabetta (3). Lucia wants one of the objects, but Alessio does not agree (3) and decides to turn his would-be partners into victims by shooting at them. He tries to get them to face him and insults them when they refuse (4). He gives up, but then seems to understand that to have somebody share in the game it is necessary to provide the objects; so he returns to Lucia and Elisabetta ready to give them other bowling pins. A third girl, Angela, approaches and asks to take part in the game, quickly showing by her remark—*Alessio, guns, Alessio*—that she understands the game. Following some talk about the distribution of the bowling pins, Alessio and Angela start shooting. Once again, as in Example 1, there are detailed instructions on the proper way of working the pretense (8). The bowling pins have to be held against the eyes and not against the chest, and the proper sound is *Pam, pam* or *Pa, pa* but not *Doo, doo.* Alessio is as attentive to these details as Angela is willing to adopt them. Similar to Example 1, it seems as if, without this very careful reproduction of all the details, the pretense of transforming a bowling pin into a gun would dissolve. The activity is repeated several times by Alessio and Angela. A little later they want to get the other two girls who still have one pin each to join in (9). Angela especially tries to convince them and, when they refuse, turns them into victims by shooting them (10). Alessio is quite indignant at their refusal and when they actually move off utters a harsh moral judgment, which is immediately repeated by Angela (11).

Example 2.2

There's the Boat and the Oars

In this sequence, which immediately followed Example 2.1, the same two children, Alessio and Angela, start a new pretend play with a new transformation of the bowling pins. The two sequences are nevertheless closely similar, not only on account of players and props being identical, but also on account of similarities in the development of the theme and the children's negotiations.

12) Alessio and Angela get onto the swing that the other two girls have abandoned. As he gets on, Alessio says: *Let's go. Where are we going? It's the boat.* And as he sits down he repeats: *We're going on the boat.* He then pretends to row using one of his bowling pins and, leaning outward, adds: *Let's row.*

Angela sits down next to Alessio and also pretends to row with a bowling pin. Alessio stops her and pointing to the far side of the swing says: *You go to that side there.* Angela moves over and pretends to row imitating Alessio's movements.

13) While the two children are rowing, Danilo (3;0) approaches and wants a place on the swing. A lively sequence ensues in which Alessio and Angela accept Danilo on the swing but want him to take part in the rowing. Danilo's refusal to accept the bowling pin that Alessio tries to give him is met with indignation. Angela passes harsh judgment on Danilo: *You're just a big bady!* [*cattivone* in Italian] *You don't have an oar!* followed by Alessio: *Cattivone . . . that's all you are!* and he continues with a word play: *Danilone, cattivone!* Things become even more serious when Danilo starts shoving the swing and disturbing the two children who had gone back to rowing. Danilo is chased off.

14) Angela stops rowing and gets off the swing. Alessio's alarm is immediate: *Where are you going?* Angela's reply, *A nanni,* could not be interpreted. Once she is off the swing, she picks up one of the bowling pins she had lost. Alessio asks again: *Where? Into the sea?* Angela walks up to him and with an *Eh?* seeks clarification. Alessio repeats: *Into the sea? Into the sea? Hey?* Angela, negative, shakes her head. Alessio: *Well then get onto the boat.* Angela goes back onto the boat with her bowling pins, sits down and looks at Alessio without saying anything. Alessio mutters something incomprehensible (*My cousin . . .*) and then goes back to rowing. Angela asks: *But where is the sea?* Alessio replies in positive tones: *Well then, row like this.*

15) Next, Danilo returns, but no sooner does he sit on the swing than he is chased off by Alessio, for Danilo won't participate in the pretense: *You don't row. No rowing for you because you're not a rower!* Alessio tells him, inventing the word "remone" for rower. Danilo moves off.

One by one, other children approach and Alessio explains the theme to each: *This is the boat!* but none of them agree to take part. In the end, one of the girls with a decided air gets onto the swing and succeeds in engaging Angela in other themes of conversation and play. Alessio then also gives up the boat theme.

In this second part of the episode the theme is again fairly simple, this time with two transformations, the boat and the oars. Again, it is Alessio who proposes and Angela who immediately accepts the theme. The disposition of the rowers and the technique (leaning out) is quickly indicated by Alessio and also accepted by Angela (12). Again as in Example 2.1, the participation of other children is dependent on their accepting the pretend theme; a moral judgment is passed on those that refuse (13). To rub it in, Alessio even invents a word (15). Angela, who accepted all the conditions, is required to remain within the fiction when she wants out (*Where are you going? Into the sea?*) (14). Because she is apparently incapable of giving a within-frame justification, she once more submits to Alessio's will. The link between the theme and the course of the pretend episode stands out in Example 2.2 because the place where the children come together is an intrinsic part of the pretend theme. The transformation of the swing into a boat is made plain by the children's activities: It is a boat because the children row in it.

In the two episodes that make up this observation the children adopt transformations that are closely linked to the physical dimensions of the objects. The bowling pins, which are long and tapering, are easily imagined to be oars; the swing with its unstable balance and on which several can sit at the same time easily becomes a boat for children used to playing at the seaside. Even if the transformations are simple, they always seem to depend on some very precise way of dealing with them, and anybody who wants to take part has to have the necessary objects. This is clear in Example 2.1 where the play is simply to perform a symbolic action with the transformed object. That possession of the object is necessary for participation is also apparent in Example 2.2, where Danilo's refusal to participate is elaborated by Angela who points out that he does not have the right object for playing: *You're just a big baby. You don't have an oar* (13). Inversely, possession of the object implies participation. On this point, serious disagreement arises in Example 2.1, when two children simply keep the objects without participating. Accepting the theme imposes constraints: It implies accepting to play and accepting how to play. When Angela no longer wants to play, she is asked to justify herself within terms of the pretend theme. Not being able to do so, she re-enters the pretense.

A particular point of Example 2.2 is the relationship between participation and meeting place. The swing space is an attraction and a meeting place for the children. The space can be divided into parts (in, out of, on, around the swing) and determines the activities of the participants. Because the swing itself becomes a transformed object, acceptance of the theme and participation are mutually reinforcing.

Example 3

From One Cake to the Next

The following gives an account of a lengthy episode made up of four sequences and characterized by the participation of a number of children at different times and in different parts of the yard.

Example 3.1

We'll Make a Cake

1) The observer approaches Simona (3;2) who has a doll under her arm and is carrying in her hand a tambourine filled with leaves and covered by a transparent plastic lid. Close by, a boy, Andrea (3;3), is handling a pair of sunglasses. Simona announces: *Let's make a cake. Eh!* and: *There you are!* She throws the doll to the ground and sits down repeating: *Let's make a cake! Eh!* Andrea follows and hunkers down next to her. He puts his hand into the tambourine on Simona's knees and with her repeats: *Let's make a cake. Eh!* Simona pushes the little boy's hand: *Go away!* and throwing the plastic cover to the ground she starts pressing the leaves in the tambourine saying: *Oh, what a lovely cake!* Another girl, Ambra (3;2), approaches and watches Simona attentively.

2) Simona places the tambourine next to her on the sidewalk and says: *We'll stick in the little candles.* She proceeds to pick blades of grass and to spread them out in front of her. In a low voice she repeats to Andrea: *There are the little candles.* With great care she several times places blades of grass on the leaves in the tambourine. Andrea repeats: *Let's make a cake* and also picks blades of grass saying: *Here. . . we'll put a lot of little candles.* Twice Simona lifts the tambourine and blows into it, then sets it down in front of her again. Andrea puts a few blades of grass into the tambourine and says in a small insistent voice: *Little caaandles, little caaandles.* The children continue arranging grass and leaves in the tambourine while Ambra still looks on attentively. Then Simona smiles, claps her hands—feebly imitated by Andrea—and says: *Good.*

3) Simona starts taking the grass out of the tambourine and, again pressing the leaves, announces: *I'm washing.* Andrea asks *Why?*, to which Simona replies: *Because.* Andrea points to the leaves in the tambourine and asks another

question: *Are they dirty?* Simona: *I want to wash.* She raises the tambourine as if she were filling it with water from some invisible source and then puts the tambourine back in front of her.

4) Sabina (2;9) comes up to Simona and Andrea, and tries to take the leaves out of the tambourine. Simona and Andrea try to stop her, but Sabina hits Andrea. In the ensuing fight, Ambra joins in on Sabina's side, and there is considerable confusion as Andrea continues to fight Ambra and Sabina. Francesca (3;1) appears and wants Andrea's glasses. She chases Ambra and Sabina away.

5) Simona, who quietly continued to manipulate the leaves in her tambourine, is now approached by another little boy, Alfredo (3;0), who asks her: *Will I give you the water?* Simona holds out her hand. Alfredo goes up to a window of the day-care building and pretends to take water from the lock of the shutter. Simona cries out to him from afar: *Leaves also, there are not enough.* Alfredo returns pretending to be carrying something in his cupped hands. Simona holds out her tambourine into which he pretends to pour what he has been holding. In the meantime, Andrea has given his glasses to Francesca and stands motionless watching her as she handles them.

Here the theme is rather complex. No longer is it simply a question of adopting one or two transformations of some object but of re-enacting a scene from daily life—in this example, the making of a birthday cake. The development of the theme brings successive transformations of related objects: The tambourine full of leaves becomes the cake, the blades of grass become little candles, and the lock of a shutter becomes a faucet. Regarding this last transformation, it seems that all the children know and understand that a particular point in space can be used for purposes of symbolization. Observing the children over a certain period of time in the day-care center, we noted that fairly frequently and in different connections the children used certain places on the wall of the day-care building, such as the locks of the shutters, as if they were supply points for food and especially for water.

The theme "making a cake" is initiated by Simona and immediately adopted by Andrea (1). The next steps, putting on the candles and clapping hands (2), are also initiated by Simona and again followed by Andrea. By contrast, the sudden change to "washing" introduced by Simona (3) is not grasped by Andrea who wants to know why. The message is, however, understood and accepted by Alfredo: he fetches some symbolic water to serve Simona, who immediately involves Alfredo apparently in the cake theme by asking him to bring more leaves (5). The sequence comes to an end when the group is broken up by the fight between Andrea, Sabina and Ambra, followed by Andrea giving his glasses to Francesca.

Example 3.2

Happy Birthday!

In the meantime, Ambra and Sabina, who were chased away by Frances-ca, get together a few feet away.

6) They sit down on the sidewalk, each with a doll under her arm. Sabina holds on her knees the plastic lid previously abandoned by Simona, and the two little girls fill it with blades of grass.

7) Ambra says to Sabina: *We put the little candles. . . let's do. . .* and she puts her hand to her mouth as if to help her blow out the candles. She pulls up blades of grass and repeats: *Little candles. . .* Sabina does not respond and, at-tracted by Andrea's glasses lying on the grass, picks them up and, turning to the other children, says: *They are glasses.* She lets the glasses drop. Ambra tells her: *They belong to those children there next to you. . .Andrea,* while she continues to pull up blades of grass. Sabina insists and pointing to the other children says: *Let's go there.* Ambra does not react and, continuing her activity, starts gently singing: *Happy birthday to you, happy birthday to you,* while beating time with her hand. But Sabina is definitely attracted by the other children now surrounding Simona who is handling the glasses. General attention is directed to what Simona is doing with the glasses, which in the end get broken.

Two children who observed what Andrea and Simona were doing but did not participate in the play now take up the theme of the birthday cake. Sabina holds one of the objects, the plastic cover handled earlier by Simona. The two girls start making the cake and fill the cover with blades of grass. The older of the two, Ambra, who observed Andrea and Simona closely, proposes to add the candles as they did and to blow them out, and adds the new idea of singing happy birthday (7). Neither proposal is taken up by Sabina, whose attention is attracted by what the other children are doing with the glasses. Finally, Am-bra also joins that group.

Example 3.3

Cooking, Eating, Spitting

The birthday cake theme continued for another 6 minutes, but without Am-bra and Sabina who went off. Certain details were left aside, new elements were added. The initiators of the pretend play, Simona and Andrea, separat-ed to pursue the theme each with another partner (Francesca and Alfredo), and later do so together once again.

8a) Simona again presses the grass inside the tambourine. Alfredo comes and tries to put his hand inside it, but Simona pushes him away, saying, in quick succession: *I give it to you, I gave it to you, me, I gave it to you.* [The imperfect tense is often used by Italian-speaking children during pretend play as the description of a hypothetical event: Let's pretend I give it to you.] She holds a blade of grass towards him; Alfredo takes it and pretends to eat. Shortly afterward, he goes away, and Simona begins to feed two dolls that were left by Ambra. But Ambra sees her, and immediately says: *Those are mine!* The two girls then walk along the building, Simona with her ''cake'' and Ambra with her two dolls.

[Simultaneously another scene is being played by Andrea and Francesca.]

8b) Francesca pretends to pour the contents of a mug over Simona's head (who does not even bother looking at her). Andrea tries to obtain the mug from Francesca, saying: *No, that goes with the cake!* Francesca runs away, followed by Andrea who asks: *You'll give me the mug?* He then shows Francesca the lock of a nearby shutter and explains: *I have to put it . . . the water, water into the cake.*

9) After a while Francesca gives in, and Andrea takes the mug. He runs back toward the shutter and pretends to get water, saying: *Shhhh,* then repeats the action quickly at two locks of the shutter, at a stand pipe along the wall, and at another window with shutters. Carefully holding the mug upright, he runs toward Simona saying: *Water, I give you water!* and pretends to pour the contents of the mug into the tambourine. He then tries to take the tambourine, but Simona refuses, saying severely: *No, it's me that does the cooking!* For a short while the children quarrel, because Simona will not let Andrea touch the tambourine.

10) Andrea then bends down to look at the hollow cylindrical support for a large umbrella and putting his hand inside says: *It needs a bit of salt.* Next he goes back to Simona with his hand stretched out and pretends to put salt into the tambourine saying: *Sh-sh.* Simona responds: *It does not matter,* but then follows him to the hollow support and asks, apparently with great interest: *Is there any salt?* Again Andrea pretends to grasp some salt and, pouring it into the tambourine, says: *Salt.* Simona stirs the grass in her tambourine and then wants to help herself to salt, but Andrea stops her and removes her hands: *No!* Once more drawing salt from the cylinder, Andrea tells Simona to bring the tambourine close to him. Simona pretends to take something out of Andrea's hand, but then pours it into the hollow of the support and manages thereby to get close to the support.

11) Andrea picks up the mug again and says in a delicately coaxing voice: *Put it in the little mug,* which he follows up with: *And you'll give me a bit of the cake, afterwards.* Seeing that Simona does not answer and that quite a small boy, Alessio, has come up asking for cake, Andrea addresses Simona again: *Give Alessio a little bit of cake.* Simona says: *OK* and puts a few blades of grass from the tambourine into the mug held by Alessio: *There you are.* Andrea renews his request: *And for me?* Simona: *Hold it, I haven't got the other mugs.* Andrea stretches his hand wide open to Simona: *Put it here, right in my own hand.* So Simona hands

Andrea some grass: *Take it.* Andrea takes it, handles it, and then puts it into the hollow of the umbrella stand. Again he asks Simona: *Give me another little bit.* Simona consents, and the scene is repeated several times until Simona notices that her tambourine is almost empty. Then Andrea lifts the grass he has in his hand to his mouth saying: *You gave it to us. Yummy!* and pretends to eat. Simona in turn also brings some grass to her mouth and then actually proceeds to eat it, is immediately disgusted and spits it out. She bursts out laughing, looks at Andrea and continues to spit. Andrea holds out some more grass to her saying: *Eat,* but she runs away. To Andrea and Alessio, who have followed her, she explains, *I have to cook it, I told you.* She proceeds to stir the contents of her tambourine. After a little while the children go to the fence that encloses the yard and tear out leaves to refill the tambourine.

The initial theme of making a cake, which in Examples 3.1 and 3.2 became making a birthday cake, is again taken up in the preceding sequence. In the action between Simona and Alfredo, and in Simona's solitary play with the dolls (8a), new elements—handing out cake as something to be eaten—are introduced. The water idea, initiated by Alfredo in Example 3.1, is taken up by Francesca (who, however, acting within a different frame, seems to be giving Simona a shampoo) and by Andrea who stays within the cake-making frame (8b).

Our two main actors, Simona and Andrea, come together again for making a cake, and a long negotiation follows on who does what part of the work. The baking is claimed by Simona because she is the first owner of the tambourine (9). Bringing water and salt is Andrea's job (8b, 9, 10). Putting these ingredients in the mix is also Andrea's job, but with a kind of trick Simona takes it over.

The whole episode is rich in transformations of specific points in space: Several different spots on the windows and on the building are treated as faucets, and the hollow of a support for an umbrella becomes a large saltcellar.

The making of the cake blends over into the distribution of the cake. The latter theme arises between Simona and Alfredo (8a); it is taken up and enlarged by Andrea (11) who asks Simona to give some cake to Alessio and to himself. A further enrichment of the theme ensues by the pretense of eating the cake, giving rise to an episode characterized both by cognitive error (the fictional status of pretending to eat is not clearly realized) and by a liking for what is forbidden when Simona actually eats the grass and spits it out in a fit of laughter. In the end, the theme of "let's make a cake" is taken up again from the very beginning by the two main actors.

Example 3.4

Spit, Spit, Spit!

For technical reasons, the observation was interrupted at this point and resumed some 10 minutes later during which time the children had moved to another part of the yard.

12) Simona is kneeling on the ground and handling some leaves mixed with earth. Two other girls try to play with her, but Simona refuses. A short quarrel develops, but stops when Andrea arrives with a bowl full of earth he collected at the other side of the yard. He pours the earth on the ground next to Simona, who complains: *Look. They won't let me cook the cake!* The other girls leave, disdainfully.

13) Andrea kneels down next to Simona and holds up the bowl patiently for her to fill it with leaves and earth. Then he stands up when Simona says: *I covered the flour . . . . give some more!* Andrea shakes his head and says: *No, that's enough!* He looks at the bowl, touches the ground, and turns toward the observer: *This . . . This is for making . . . ;* he then picks up a doll that was lying close by, comes back to Simona and adds: *For this baby here.* Both children place the doll on the ground in front of the heap of earth. Simona fills the bowl held by Andrea and says: *Wait!* Andrea answers something incomprehensible and pours the contents of the bowl over the doll. Both children burst out laughing and Simona says: *Wash there!* taking a handful of earth and dripping it onto the doll's mouth.

14) Simona says: *Again!* and fills with earth the bowl that Andrea holds up in front of her. Then Andrea also starts filling the bowl. Simona says: *I want to feed the baby!* Andrea replies: *Me too!* Simona takes a handful of earth and Andrea bends over the doll and asks: *On the eyes?* Simona throws a handful of earth over the doll's head, bursts out laughing, and says: *There!* Andrea also laughs. Simona glances at him, lifts the doll up with its face downward, and says: *Spit, spit, spit!* Andrea looks on attentively. Simona puts the doll back on the ground and the two children fill the bowl again with earth.

15) The children repeat this sequence several times in perfect agreement and shared excitement. They laugh uproariously when Simona says: *Spit, spit, spit!* and take turns filling the bowl and pouring the contents over the doll's face, but only Simona turns the doll face down and pronounces the ritual words.

16) While Simona gathers more earth, Andrea holds the bowl and, pointing to the doll's head, says: *And then I turn it over.* Simona fills the bowl, lifts the doll toward Andrea who pours earth onto the doll's face: *There!* and then turns the doll's face down, whispering: *Spit, spit.* He laughs. Simona takes the doll, pours another handful of earth on its face: *There!* and starts filling the bowl again. Suddenly she lifts the doll toward Andrea, saying: *Now!* and Andrea pours earth over its face: *There! Spit, spit, spit!* and he turns the doll face down after having said the words. Simona repeats softly: *Spit, spit, spit!* Another child comes along and asks: *What you doing?* Simona answers immediately: *It's the kitchen. We are . . . . ha, ha, ha!* pretending to laugh, and lifting the doll. Andrea looks on and smiles. The two then start collecting more earth.

17) Simona lifts the doll high in the air but Andrea intervenes: *Now . . . no, here!* and with a decided air he puts the doll face down on the ground.

Simona then holds the doll on the ground and Andrea pours earth from the bowl along the doll's back, shouting excitedly: *There, there, there!* Simona takes a handful of earth and also pours it over the doll: *There, there!* then she suddenly brushes the earth away and turns the doll face upward, saying: *Spit, spit, spit!* She throws more earth on the doll's face, but Andrea pushes her hands away, cleans the doll, moves it away from Simona, and says: *No, you put it here, friend,* pointing to the bowl. Simona begins to fill the bowl again, and the two children talk (not understood). Another boy comes along and Andrea tells him: *We're doing a bit of work, throwing this* (with a gesture of turning something over) *and then . . . spit, spit, spit!* Putting his hand in front of his mouth he simulates laughter: *Ha, ha, ha!* The other child says nothing and goes away. Simona and Andrea continue to play together for a while.

In this episode, the introduction of a forbidden act (throwing earth in somebody's eyes) heightens the emotional tone of the play and may echo another forbidden act in Example 3.3 when Simona actually puts grass into her mouth. The sequence of putting earth into the bowl, pouring it over the doll's mouth, turning the doll over, and telling her to spit is repeated several times and becomes a ritual. Andrea's proposal to introduce a variation by pouring earth on the back of the doll (17) is not accepted by Simona. Andrea's description of what they are doing in answer to another child's question shows the importance for the children of a strict sequential order and especially of the final burst of laughter, which strongly suggests that the pretend play is approaching a forbidden zone.

The four sequences of Example 3 may be summarized as follows:

Example 3.1 Themes: Stirring leaves in a tambourine and adding water = preparing the cake mix. Putting blades of grass on the leaves and blowing = placing the birthday candles and blowing them out. *Objects*: Tambourine plus leaves = cake; blades of grass = candles; a lock on shutter = a faucet. Lid of the tambourine, a doll. *Main actors*: Simona, Andrea. *Helper*: Alfredo. *Observers*: Ambra, Sabina, Francesca.

Example 3.2 Themes: As in Example 3.1 except that grass has become the main ingredient and singing is now part of the celebration. *Objects*: Blades of grass = both the cake and the candles. Lid of the tambourine, dolls. *Main actors*: Ambra, Sabina.

Example 3.3 Themes: Handling the leaves or the grass in the tambourine = baking the cake. Handing out leaves = handing out cake. Bringing pretend water and salt = helping in making the cake. Hand-to-mouth of leaves and grass = eating the cake. *Objects*: As before + support for umbrella = saltcellar; doll = baby. A mug. *Main actors*: Simona and Alfredo, Andrea and Francesca, Simona and Andrea.

Example 3.4 Themes: Fill a bowl with earth, pour onto a doll, turn doll face down, and say *Spit* = giving baby something forbidden to eat. *Objects*: Earth = cake but apparently also just earth; doll = baby. A bowl. *Main actors*: Simona and Andrea. Several observers.

The elaboration of the theme from Example 3.1 to Example 3.2 is fairly simple, the participants in Example 3.2 having carefully observed what happened in Example 3.1. But with Example 3.3, when the first two principal actors take up the theme again, greater variation is introduced with other children taking part. Now the cake has to be handed out and eaten, and quite a number of new symbolizations are used, notably of certain fixed points in space. All the elements of the theme are taken up in Example 3.4, again by the first pair of children. In their new play, symbolized activity is prominent seeing that the cake no longer requires a container and that what the pretend baby is given to eat ceases to represent cake but is simply earth that has to be spat out. Elements developed in previous episodes are now combined in a pattern where symbolic aspects are merged with ritual aspects. To all this is added the element of interdiction, which increases the make-believe character of the children's play as well as their obvious enjoyment.

Yet the variations are not very many and are often not easily accepted. Every new departure entails a new division of labor as well as negotiation of the relationship between the partners: Who is going to keep the objects? Who is going to do the main or the most interesting part (e.g., who is going to say: *Spit, spit spit?*)? Looking at our two principal actors, it is clear that Simona retains the main task of manipulating the cake, a task she has had from the beginning as the possessor of the tambourine and that she maintains even when the action is reduced to simply picking up earth from the ground. Dividing the tasks is the greatest source of conflict between the children: According to Simona, Andrea should restrict himself to bringing ingredients or to merely helping with making the cake, for example by holding the bowl (Example 3.4). By contrast, they are in easy agreement regarding the development of the theme. It is interesting to note that most of the children who just occasionally enter the game seem fully conscious of what is going on.

Throughout Example 3, the children use points fixed in space in two different ways. On the one hand, certain spots are identified as supply points for cake-making ingredients; on the other, space is used as a kind of psychological distance between activities; for example in Example 3.4, when Sabina is preparing the cake in one spot, Andrea goes to fetch earth somewhere else.

The examples show that pretend play flourishes even in places not specially equipped for the purpose. Activities from everyday life, well known to all the children, are re-enacted, but there are also less commonplace themes such as the shooting in Example 2. These do not belong to two distinct categories seeing that even in everyday scenes, as in Example 3.4, the children introduce unusual elements such as *Spit spit spit.* Because adequate props are not present, all episodes call for symbolic transformations of objects and places.

Several children take part in all the episodes and accordingly there has to be a sharing of symbols: Transformations are proposed that may be accepted, modified, or refused; and this depends on both the requirements of the theme and the desires of the individual participants.

Most of the observed pretend episodes were lengthy (up to 45 minutes) and many spread over all the space available in the yard. A theme was often picked up unchanged, or was modified or commented upon by different groups of children and at different times as part of a social dynamism that reached beyond the children actually taking part in the pretense. The yard, as a large communal space, brought out the collective aspects of the children's activities, favored the continual merging and dispersal of small groups of children, and provided a variety of anchorages for special symbolizations.

SYMBOLIZATION AND THEME DEVELOPMENT

Whereas in Examples 1 and 2 the theme depends on the transformation of objects, the central theme of Example 3 concerns an everyday activity to which the transformed objects are subordinated.

In Example 1, the transformation is limited to pretending that a toy boat has a siren that can be worked by pressure on a certain spot. In Example 2, where movement and sound also go together, the fiction is more elaborate by one step: The bowling pin has been transformed into a gun. Suggestive of a gun, the pin is also suggestive of an oar, although symbolizing an oar is subordinate to the swing becoming a boat. The children's capacity to extend the play theme inferentially, even if the theme was originally proposed by somebody else, is shown, for example, in the idea that if you shoot with a gun then a person who opposes the shooter's desires becomes a target. Similarly, being on the swing, using bowling pins, and getting down onto the grass is coherently transformed into being on a boat, rowing with the oars, and getting into the water. In Example 3, most of the transformations of objects are not so much related to actions evoked by either the objects or their symbols, but are subordinate to a central, everyday activity. Other transformations (lock = faucet) seem not to depend on the actual theme but to be part of what all the children know.

In all our observations, certain objects play a pivotal role in theme development and role distribution (e.g., the plastic boats, the bowling pins, the tambourine, the bowl). Space also plays an important part: The swing space is a meeting point for the children, and whoever goes there is solicited to participate in the play. The swing itself is given a symbolic meaning. Space is also used to determine different activities: In the cake-making observation, preparing the mix is not done in the same place as gathering the ingredients.

The children's attention and their discussions are centered on particular aspects of the pretense, depending on the status of the symbolic transformations introduced. In Examples 1 and 2.1, great attention is paid to the precise manner in which the siren and the guns are to be manipulated. In Example 2.2, the consistency of activities within the symbolic frame is discussed (because the swing is a boat, you can't step out of it onto the grass, you jump into the water). Both the attention to detail and the demand for coherence appear to indicate that the children are aware of the constraints implied by sharing symbolic meanings in collective pretense.

Example 3 is based on a well-known activity, and the children's discussions do not concern the manner in which the symbolized objects should be handled, but the introduction of new elements and who should play which part. In the final episode, however, when the well-known theme is changed into a new ritual, sequence and manner become important once more (on what part of the doll the earth should be thrown, how to hold the doll, and when to say *Spit spit spit*).

The theme and its development are thus closely linked to the different interacting and negotiating patterns that were observed.

PROPAGATION OF THEMES

A theme may be transmitted directly from one child to another or to several children. This happens when a child gives or asks for a pivotal object (Examples 1 and 2) or when a pivotal object happens to devolve on a possible partner (the lid of the tambourine in Example 3.2). At other times, a theme may develop among children engaged in some other activity (Examples 1.1, 3.1, 3.4) or when a child explicitly asks to be included (Example 3.3). Frequently, however, the propagation of pretend themes takes place indirectly. In Example 1, several children watch Lorenzo and Marco, and then join in the boat play; in Example 3.2, Ambra and Sabina take up the theme they saw played by Simona and Andrea. In both these observations, the new participants possess either another exemplar of the pivotal object (a plastic boat) or a part of such an object (the lid of the tambourine), and only later introduce some variation into the original scenario. Alfredo, however, who observed the first part of the cake-making play, immediately proposes something new when he joins in (adding water to the mix). Not all the interested observers want to take part; in Example 3, several children come to watch Simona and Andrea, who, apparently aware of the attention, occasionally explain what is going on, but the others depart. Some themes are developed over a long time in various locations and by different groups of children, who introduce new elements and sometimes, as in Example 3, change the character of the pretense.

CONCLUDING REMARKS

Although Piaget did not study collective pretend play in detail, he in no way depreciated its importance. The analyses presented in this chapter are focused on sociocognitive aspects of pretend play; in Piaget's (1976b) words: "There are collective pretend scenarios, with the participants taking up roles that become gradually differentiated and that are often carefully regulated during the development of the pretense. . . . These play sequences present the interest of establishing a socialization of affective aspects . . . of the children's lives as well as a socialization of symbolic thinking" (p. 192). In his study of the game of marbles, Piaget's (1932/1932) interest was focused on the development of mutual respect and collaboration, and, in his observations of symbolic play of children playing alone, his main object was the study of mental representation in the areas in which "the individual processes of mental life dominate the collective factors" (Piaget, 1945/1951, p. 2). Nonetheless, on the relations between different types of play, the two works in question contain a number of observations and speculations that are consonant with the results of our studies of collective pretend play. Four points stand out.

1. From the age of about 8 months onward, the motor schemes engender a kind of empty functioning in which the infant takes pleasure as if playing. J. (10 months), in her bath, rubs her hair and then slaps the water with her hands. During the next few days this sequence becomes ritualized to the extent that she no longer slaps the water without first sketching a movement of rubbing her hair, a game that amuses her by its very regularity (Piaget, 1932/1932, p. 22). Such sequences are taken out of their original context, and become pretense (e.g., pretending to be asleep) and lead to the construction of symbols. Pretend play begins by a simple action, and somewhat later incorporates substitute objects (Piaget, 1945/1951, pp. 94–97).

2. Piaget (1932/1932, p. 43) noted that for very young children there is as yet no differentiation between the rules of a ritual they invent themselves, regularities that are due to physical causality, and moral rules that grow out of mutual respect. Neither the pleasure the child takes in regularities (observable in the joy with which children between the ages of one and two reproduce certain behaviors in great detail), nor the beginning awareness of the rules they follow lead directly toward the ability of school-age children to play rule games, in which some idea of binding agreement is necessary (Piaget, 1932/1932, pp. 22–23). The psychological status of rules changes profoundly, in line with general sociocognitive development. The change is gradual and begins early: "As soon as a ritual is established by two children in collaboration, it acquires in the conscience of the subject a new aspect, precisely that of a rule. This aspect may vary according to the dominant type of respect between the partners (respect for an older child, or mutual respect) but in both cases an element

of submission appears which was absent from the simple ritual'' (Piaget, 1932/1932, p. 23).

3. Sharing a ludic ritual does not immediately lead to collective symbolism. Piaget gave an example of two children (below the age of 3) in which the actions of the older are imitated by the younger child, but without the two giving the same symbolic meanings to the actions. ''One observes how totally devoid of any general direction are the ritualized action schemes successively tried. But as soon as there is reciprocal imitation, we have the beginning of a rule'' (Piaget, 1932/1932, p. 20). Collective symbolism is elaborated by children from the age of about 4 through ''the differentiation and adjustment of roles'' (Piaget, 1945/1951, p. 138). Like on many other occasions, Piaget emphasized that it is impossible to find a causal link between social and mental acquisitions as they are two aspects of the same development, ''this organized collective symbolism implies progress towards order and coherence. . . .But it could equally well be maintained that coherence of thought comes from progress in socialization'' (Piaget, 1945/1951, p. 139).

4. ''There is something more in the collective rule than in the motor rule or the individual ritual, just as there is something more in the *signe* than in the *symbole*'' (Piaget, 1932/1932, p. 23). Adopting the terminology of de Saussure, Piaget (1945/1951, p. 98) made a distinction between conventional and arbitrary *signes* such as words and *symboles*, so-called motivated signifiers that are related to their signified by some resemblance, and may be the product of individual thought. ''In the case of ludic symbols we must note that progress in socialization, instead of leading to an increase in symbolism, transforms it more or less rapidly into objective imitation of reality'' (Piaget, 1945/l951, p. 139).

Piaget's hypotheses appear to be corroborated by the results of our analyses and to throw light on the intricate relations between the social and cognitive components of collective pretend play.

In the first place, regarding the social aspects, we observed agreements (or negotiations in order to arrive at an agreement) about the contents to be symbolized, driven by the children's desire to share a pretend episode with others, or, more simply, to do as the others do. We also observed their efforts to combine the intentions of different children within one play frame. It would appear that such nascent collective symbolism can favor social and cognitive development, because it contributes to the decrease of egocentrism (defined by Piaget, 1932/1932, p. 87, as a confusion between the self and the milieu, and as a lack of collaboration). Indeed, the dissociation between the self and the group (or the outer world in general) as well as the convergence of one's own ideas and desires with those of others may be easier to realize in collective pretend play than in individual thinking. Shared ludic symbols certainly have a psychological status that is different from subjective symbols: especially when they are established by negotiations, refusals, and final agreements, they contribute to the dissociation between self and others, and lead to collaboration.

In the second place, on the cognitive level, it appears that there is as yet no clear differentiation between sharing play rituals, awareness of rules, and collective symbolism. We observed strong feelings of obligation that certain actions had to be performed "just so." This phenomenon presents various aspects.

Physical causality and rules of play are not yet clearly differentiated: Rules of play appear as rigid as the ideas of children at this age about physical causality. We suppose that, precisely through collective pretend play, children will become aware of the difference between the regularities of phenomena of physical causality and the consistency necessary for collective symbolic thought.

In our observations, the way a theme is enacted takes on an obligatory character such that it has to be faithfully repeated, especially when a symbolic transformation is implied. Apparently, only the exact reproduction of symbolic meanings in action is a guarantee of their existence and their conservation.

Both the meaning of the game and the pleasure it gives depend on regularity of action. We often saw how concerned children were with reproducing an activity exactly, and how such concern influenced their interaction: "to do as the others do" became "this is the way one does it" or even "this is way one has to do it." The same phenomenon was observed (Musatti & Panni, 1981) with infants of less than 18 months during motoric play: The exact reproduction of movements was clearly a "ritual" obligation for the group. In collective play, the necessity to repeat the same actions in order to make their playful character clear is confused with the need to imitate someone else's actions in order to share the other's pleasure and playful intentions. Indeed, the dividing line between sharing a play ritual and beginning to construct the rules of a game is not easy to draw. We observed many instances of quasi-magical rule observance in the pretend play of our subjects; what distinguishes such rules from those that older children follow in their games is that the older children are aware of certain moral norms and of the rules having been established and accepted by the players themselves.

In early individual pretend play, as described by Piaget (1945/1951), play rituals lead to symbolism via a process of conventionalization. In collective pretend play, the transformation of a ritual into a rule and its conventionalization into a shared symbolism are closely linked. In Example 3.4, this appears clearly: The two children share the symbolic transformation of their play ritual and can communicate the rules governing their activity.

The phenomenon of spatiotemporal propagation reminds us of Piaget's (1963, reprinted 1976a) remark that "social constraints do not do away with symbolic thought, but crystallize and consolidate it" (p. 102). All societies construct collective symbolic representations (myths, rites, patriotic ceremonies, etc). Symbolic thought, defined by reference to its differences with rational thought, retains its force. Even if symbolic thought declines in technologically advanced societies, it remains an important element in social communication. The pretend-play symbols we observed could well be early examples of the crystallization and consolidation of symbolic thought in the microsociety of the daycare center. During our observations of pretend play in the yard, where about 40 children congregated, we noted an as yet limited number of play symbols and pieces of knowledge shared by this small community. Through conventionalization, this shared knowledge can be used implicitly for communication. Two aspects, however, differentiate these exchanges during pretend play from the communication of more strictly objective knowledge. First, the shared symbols remain fairly idiosyncratic, because they are valid only within the specific community. Second, the symbols the children construct (such as the symbolic transformation of an object) remain totally attached to the pretend-play activity and derive their meaning from that activity. The shared knowledge, created and conventionalized by the children themselves, is added to the conventional shared knowledge about social life in the world of adults (Garvey, 1982; Nelson & Seidman, 1984) and enriches as well as facilitates interindividual understanding, but only in the context of pretend play. In this sense, shared play symbols appear, in the formation of young children's representational system, to be intermediate between the individual pole and the social pole.

The socialization process of young children thus seems to comprise microphenomena suggesting a similarity between the conventionalization of symbolic elements in shared play and the creation of collective symbolisms that are part of the culture of any community. We observed such processes to be at work in social relationships (creation of rituals leading to rules) and in the organization of knowledge (creation of sets of shared meanings). The phenomena reported appear to constitute a beginning of child folklore, although still restricted to the small community of the center. Authors who have studied the child folklore phenomenon (Moore & Young, 1979; Opie & Opie, 1959; Osorina, 1986) found certain characteristic elements that were observed also in our study; a privileged status of outdoor space, the attribution of meaning to particular points in space, the creation of rituals and of a shared repertoire of fantasy including songs, quasi-magical ceremonies, and rhythmical and rhyming storytelling. Because the increasing number of centers where very young children come together offer many occasions for observing early socialization processes, one may expect as yet unknown aspects of the links between cognitive development, socialization in peer groups and cultural integration to be brought to light.

ACKNOWLEDGMENTS

We are grateful to the children of the day-care center Via Boito, Comune di Roma, for their inventive play and to the staff of the center for their valuable collaboration.

Chapter 3

Negotiations Among Children and Pretend Play*

Laura Bonica
Università di Genova

This chapter presents the analysis of one lengthy pretend-play episode, with special reference to the transformation of interpersonal relationships between children during their construction of the pretense. The main theme of the episode is giving food to a baby, a cat, another child. In pretend situations with asymmetrical roles (e.g., mother–baby, teacher–pupil), relationships between the partners are often uncertain because each child has to distinguish the pretend role to be played from possible roles in real life. Symmetrical roles (e.g., parents looking after a baby, several people preparing a picnic) are easier; but in both cases ambiguities arise in the communication between partners: Does one speak in one's own name, as a child, or as a character in the pretense? Does the discussion concern the question of who will direct the play or of what the theme is going to be?

Various communicative strategies are used by the children to unravel ambiguous situations and to deal with complications that may arise. These strategies aim at reestablishing equilibrated interaction. To negotiate means to confer with one another for the purpose of reaching agreement, and implies the existence of discord or misunderstanding. Yet, it is not always clear whether the desired agreement concerns the play (its theme and development) or the personal relations between the partners (their reciprocal acceptance as individuals).

From this point of view, transitions between agreement and conflict as well as processes of dissociation between self and others are of particular interest,

---

*This chapter is based on observations made in a day-care center in Genoa.

and their study should clarify the function of pretend play in the regulation of interpersonal relations: In what ways is collective pretense a source of conflict, and in what ways is it a means of resolving conflict?

Our analyses are partly based on work by Wallon (1949) and Bateson (1955). In particular, Wallon's view on the differentiation between self and others is important for our analyses. Like Piaget, he attributed to the social group the role of an indispensable intermediary for the construction of reciprocal respect between persons; but Wallon assigned greater weight to society in the construction of the self and the construction of knowledge than did Piaget. "For human beings, society is a necessity, an organic reality . . . the individual . . . tends towards society as towards an equilibrium" (Wallon, 1949, p. 8). Society functions on the one hand as a source of conflict and on the other as a mediating influence leading to the resolution of conflict. The very young child alternates between a kind of fusion with others and disengagement. The infant's sensitivity to others is clearly visible in what Wallon (1949, p. 127) called "the reaction of deportment": Infants show postural changes when they notice somebody observing them. This behavior announces an awareness of one's self as a person who is influenced by the presence of others and who can influence the behavior of others.

The first phase of the differentiation between self and others is based on individual emotional contrasts (pleasure–displeasure) and on interpersonal relationships (demand–submission). Gradually, children become capable of identifying both the persons with whom and the situation in which they interact. According to Wallon (1949, p. 115), from about the age of 3 they begin to understand that interpersonal relationships may change when the situation changes. But at this age, such understanding is still fragile and does not exclude violent opposition to others, which serves self-affirmation and thereby contributes to the construction of the self. Wallon explained such opposition as the result of an incapacity to understand that people's roles and attitudes are not permanent, but depend on the situation. In order to understand this nonpermanence in oneself and in others, and to construct a self that can adjust to others' desires without losing its identity, it is necessary to interact with others who can function as a mirror of oneself.

Bateson (1955) was the first to emphasize the need for signaling the switch from real-life identity to pretend identity in make-believe play. Similarly, he and his followers (cf. Watzlawick, Beavin, & Jackson, 1967) argued that every communicative act not only serves to provide information on the content and theme of a conversation, but also, at another level of abstraction, to specify the nature of the interpersonal relationship between the participants. The existence of two levels of communication may lead to contradictions when the verbal utterances do not correspond to the accompanying nonverbal communications, which may remain unconscious for the speaker, but are taken into account and interpreted by the addressee. Each communicative act thus pertains to the content of the conversation as well as to the interpersonal relationship between the partners. If the partners agree on both levels of communication, their shared activity develops in a harmonious and productive manner. If there is disagreement, there may be a contradiction between the two levels, which the discussants will have to clarify. In moments of conflict and during negotiation, the differentiation between the two levels becomes crucial, and it is often the interpersonal relationship that emerges as the most important element, even if the partners appear to continue to discuss the content.

Varied information can be transmitted at the relational level:

- agreement or disagreement (you are right or you are wrong),
- valorization or devalorization (I accept you as a valid interlocutor, as a person who can have thoughts, intentions, and feelings that can influence somebody else or I don't accept you as such),
- double bind or paradoxical injunction (I express contradictory sentiments so that you cannot understand whether I agree or not).

In negotiations, the participants' main preoccupation is to defend the integrity of their internal self. Each utterance by one of the participants in the dialogue is thus interpreted by the other according to the degree of danger or reassurance it may represent for his or her security. Each utterance also contributes to the clarification of the relationship (as more or less symmetrical or complementary) as well as to the meaning of various changes in the objective content of the exchange. The interpersonal dimension is thus always present, even if there is no conflict and if for the observer this aspect seems absent. When the interpretations made by the participants are consonant, this equilibrium at the level of the relationship allows smooth progress in the dialogue, even if content is difficult. Conflict may arise during negotiation over interpreting the content of an utterance or at the interpersonal level. When emotional security is threatened, the object of the negotiation becomes the relationship, and its aim the reestablishment of interpersonal equilibrium. When the participants want to stay together, they have to face the problem of a change in inter- and intrapersonal conditions. Strategies used for modifying the interpersonal situation may then interfere with the content of the negotiation, and this is where the partner's ability to understand the level of communication is crucial. From this point of view, conflicts, and the manner in which they are resolved, are particularly apt to reveal regulatory processes in interpersonal relations (cf. Bonica, 1986, 1987). Therefore, the analyses reported in this chapter bear mainly on moments of interruption and conflict in collective pretend play, when complex interpersonal negotiations take place. The observations raise a number of questions. What strategies are used by our 3-year-old subjects to avoid disrupting their play? How does the transition from one episode to another take place? Do their negotiations show two levels of communication (a) concerning the content of the pretense, and (b) concerning their interpersonal relations? How do they deal with ambiguities that arise in certain scenarios where the distribution of roles calls for clear distinction between a pretend relationship and a real, direct relationship? Because the differentiation between self and others is supposed to attain a certain level at the age of 3, can negotiations in pretend play reveal progress in this domain?

To provide some answers to these questions, 10 videorecordings of approximately 1 hour each were selected from a large number obtained in several day-care centers; these recordings were made whenever small groups of 3-year-olds started a pretend episode. In most groups, there were four or five children, boys as well as girls, and the pretend play took place in a "kitchen corner," equipped with dishes, pots, dolls, and so on. The analysis of the observations centered on the links between the various phases of a pretend-play episode, its start, the first proposals, explicit or implicit proposals for a change of theme, momentary disruptions, and the effect of changes in attitude. Phases that most clearly revealed processes of negotiation and of differentiation between self and others were analyzed in detail, as in the example (given later) of one episode between two girls, joined occasionally by some other children. This episode was chosen because it incorporates most of the phenomena observed in the large number of tapes at our disposal. Interaction between the two girls illustrates the many communicative strategies used by children at this age in order to establish a basis for equilibrated exchanges that will allow play to develop and continue.

The entire episode is presented and commented upon; the discussion is mainly based on this one extensive example, although occasionally other observations are referred to when they can throw additional light on the negotiating process and the changes of interpersonal relationships that lead to reciprocal adjustment. The episode is divided into four phases. These phases and the children's verbal and nonverbal interactions are analyzed step by step; a more general interpretation based on explanatory hypotheses is presented in the discussion. The four phases are as follows:

Phase 1: Initial positioning of the partners and their exploration of common zones of tolerance. This phase is characterized by ambiguities leading to misunderstanding.

Phase 2: Retroactive control processes to deal with changes in interpersonal relations. This phase is characterized by the repetition of strategies used in the first phase and by a hardening of attitudes leading to sudden changes and finally to a shut-down of rational communication.

Phase 3: Activation of self-corrective mechanisms within the interactional system. This phase is characterized by the establishment of an identity or similarity between the two partners, the clarification of the disagreement, and the resolution of the conflict through reciprocal acceptance of differences.

Phase 4: Productive negotiation and resumption of the pretense.

In the first two phases the proposed scenario engenders ambiguities that cause communication to break down. The third phase appears as an abandon of the proposed play and as a search for a way of discussing the disagreement (metanegotiation). The last phase appears as a kind of check-up of the success of the metanegotiations.

PHASE 1: INITIAL ATTITUDES
AND INTERPERSONAL EXPLORATIONS

The first phase is composed of three parts:

(1) Two girls, Silvia (3;1) and Serena (3;0), try to find a theme acceptable to both.
(2) A third child, Rocco (2;10), intervenes. His intervention helps the girls to negotiate.
(3) The negotiation is blocked by a misunderstanding and the conflict is aggravated.

1) Serena goes to the kitchen corner, where there are a small chair, some plates, cups, etc., and calls out: *Dinner is ready! Dinner is ready! Dinner is ready! Let's eat! The pap!* [pappa in Italian]. Silvia, Rocco, and Elisabeta (3;1) come toward her, and Silvia, who holds a baby doll, repeats: *Dinner is ready!*

Silvia lays her baby doll on the chair. Serena tries to take it from her, but Silvia holds on and installs the doll properly on the chair. *No, not like that, you have to do it like so,* says Serena, picking up the doll and seating it differently while Silvia looks on. Serena then puts some clothes on the doll. Silvia says: *No!* and takes the doll back, undresses it and puts on different clothes. Serena once again tries to get hold of the doll, but Silvia resists and begins to feed the baby.

Comment

Serena's proposal to play *Let's eat!* gathers three children around her. The proposed theme left many possibilities open for development. Serena probably felt encouraged by the three children joining, but Silvia's putting the doll on the chair appears to disturb her. Silvia's action is ambiguous: Is she proposing to develop the theme, or is she making a counterproposal? Serena apparently accepts Silvia's idea of including a doll in the pretense, but she wants to maintain her position as initiator and director. She tries to take possession of the doll, and assumes the role of the person who really knows what is right and proper. But Silvia resists and reasserts her authority over the doll. Their dialogue is clearly conflictual, but what is the object of the conflict? The distribution of roles in regard to the doll, or more generally the theme of the pretense (the inclusion of a doll)? Quite possibly, the conflict is interpersonal from the beginning and concerns the question of who has the right to decide on a theme.

2) While Serena is pretending to feed the doll, Rocco intervenes and asks: *Why do you give the baby to eat and to drink?* Silvia starts to answer: *Because . . . ,* but Serena interrupts her and says: *Because he's hungry. And then he'll go to bed!* Silvia listens and looks bewildered. Serena immediately takes a glass, and holds it toward Silvia, saying: *There, that's water.* Silvia takes the glass but puts it aside and picks up a baby bottle. *Why do you give him milk?* asks Serena. *Because, because he's little!* answers Silvia. Serena looks at Silvia and declares: *Now he doesn't eat any more.* Silvia caresses the doll's head and says: *Well done!*

Comment

Rocco's question leads the girls to negotiate their roles vis-à-vis the doll. Serena wants to make it clear which of the two girls directs the play and answers Rocco in Silvia's place. At one level she presents herself as Silvia's helper, but at the same time she sends Silvia a twofold message: She is ready to play at feeding the baby, as Silvia proposed, but she herself is the one who knows what the baby needs. This double message leaves Silvia bewildered. Serena profits from the situation and emphasizes her role as a specialist in baby care by handing Silvia a glass supposed to contain water. But Silvia has her own idea and gives the baby a bottle. Does she feel put down by Serena who seems to treat her as incompetent and does she want to show her knowledge about babies? Serena now changes her strategy and asks Silvia to explain her action. Silvia answers, more relaxed than before, that the baby is still very small. Serena's question indicated an interest in Silvia's doings, which may have reassured Silvia. In turn, Serena feels that she can take the lead again: *Now he doesn't eat any more.* This statement may have a double meaning: Taken as an utterance within the frame, it counts as expert advice about baby care, but it can also be taken as a proposal to change the scenario in such a way that the baby disappears from the pretend play. Silvia's answer is just as ambiguous: within the frame, she stops feeding the baby and congratulates him, but as a direct communication to Serena her action may be taken as a concession.

3) Serena picks up a pot and holds it toward Silvia, saying: *Pap.* Silvia takes it and starts to feed the doll from the pot, taking the food with her hand. Serena

blocks Silvia's hand and says: *No, no, not the pap!* Silvia asks: *But what do we give him, then?* Serena answers: *The pap!* Silvia then takes a plate, and appears to want to use it to feed the doll, but Serena takes it away from her, turns it upside down and cries: *No, no!* Silvia looks astonished, but continues to feed the doll from the pot, saying: *Eat, OK?* Serena looks irritated, stands up and sits down again between Silvia and Rocco. Silvia goes on feeding the doll.

Comment

The lack of agreement between the two girls is obvious, but their dialogue is incoherent (*No, not the pap.—What then?—The pap!*) and leads to communication being blocked. Two levels of communication are apparently confused. Silvia stays within the frame of the immediately preceding scene (feeding the doll), and, because she thinks her partner is willing to continue the theme, asks what else she should feed the doll. Serena's answer seems to indicate that she thinks Silvia agreed to change the theme and to go back to Serena's very first proposal (*Let's eat the pap*). The simple word "pap" is ambiguous with respect to the level of communication: an in-frame answer to Silvia's question or an out-of-frame proposal for a change of theme? Serena does not provide any clues that might clarify her answer, which is inconsistent with her own previous utterance. There also remains an ambiguity concerning the underlying interpersonal conflict that leads to Serena's not being satisfied with the theme proposed by Silvia.

PHASE 2: RETROACTIVE CONTROL PROCESSES TO DEAL WITH CHANGES IN INTERPERSONAL RELATIONSHIPS

This second phase is divided into four parts:

(4) Serena tries once again to dissuade Silvia from feeding the doll, but Silvia maintains her opposition.

(5) Rocco comes into the play again and provides opportunity for some positive sharing, but the occasion is short-lived.

(6) Serena takes advantage of Rocco's invitation to leave.

(7) Silvia calls back Serena. It is not easy to get the play going again.

4) Serena intervenes: *He doesn't want to swallow!* Rocco asks: *Why isn't he eating?* Even Elisabeta, who has joined in, makes some remarks: *Is he eating or is he not eating? Is he being naughty?* But Silvia ignores everybody and goes on feeding the doll.

Serena then starts tapping the doll on the back: *Eat!* just as Silvia is letting the doll drink.

Serena once again speaks to the doll: *Are you being naughty?* tapping him the while on the back. Silvia hugs the doll close and then looking at him says: *You're good! And now for the pap.*

Once again Serena tries to take the doll away from Silvia but Silvia, pursuing her idea, holds onto him and feeds him with a spoon: *How well you open your mouth wide. Great! You are hungry, aren't you?*

Comment

Serena's remark about the doll not wanting to swallow may be another attempt to restructure the theme of the pretense and a retake of when she announced that the baby was no longer eating (2). Silvia makes it quite clear that she intends to continue to play at feeding the baby and Serena once again uses the strategy of entering into this pretense via a remark about the baby's behavior. But Silvia contradicts Serena: Instead of scolding the baby, she praises him. This contradiction may at the same time signify her opposition to Serena's attempting to change the theme. What the other two children do does not help to reduce the conflict.

5) Rocco starts pretending to be a baby: *I want water, I want water!* Silvia pays no attention and continues to feed the doll. Serena answers Rocco: *No!* Rocco continues to play baby, and apparently pretends to be sick: he coughs, makes vomiting movements, and cries. Serena pays no attention to him, goes to Silvia and hands her a spoon, a plate, and a glass, to be used for the baby. For a while, the two girls play together in silence.

Comment

Rocco tries to interest the two girls in a pretense in which he would play the role of a baby. Neither of the girls is interested in this proposal, and Serena makes it clear that she wants to continue playing with Silvia. Rocco's attempt may well have resulted in bringing the two girls closer together. By helping Silvia in silence, Serena checks on Silvia being indeed ready to accept her as a helpmate, although perhaps not as an equal.

6) Rocco feels neglected, begins to ride a bicycle and speaks directly to Serena, looking at her and showing her another bicycle: *That's your bicycle!* Serena stands up, turns away from Silvia, goes toward Rocco and asks: *This one? Is that mine?* Rocco answers: *Yes, that's yours!* and he and Silvia start riding round the room on their bicycles.

Comment

Rocco finds a way of attracting Serena's attention and luring her away from Silvia. Serena accepts his invitation (Rocco said: _your bicycle_). She takes the opportunity of moving away from Silvia, probably because her efforts to take part in directing the play were unsuccessful.

7) Silvia turns to Serena and cries: _Serena! come and help me with the baby._ A little later she adds: _Or . . . he's going to cry!_ Serena immediately returns and proceeds to scold the baby: _Eat up your pasta! If you don't, you'll see what happens!_ Silvia looks at her, puzzled, and puts the baby on the chair. Serena looks on and asks quietly: _Are you putting him right?_ She starts to give the baby something to drink, but the glass slips out of her hand. She cries: _Oh! The water fell!_ Silvia intervenes immediately: _Why do you give him lemon? He does not want lemon, he does not want lemon!_

Rocco goes toward the two girls and asks: _Why doesn't he want lemon? Why doesn't he want it?_ Serena says to Rocco: _No, she doesn't give him lemon, she gives him water!_ Silvia asks: _Is it water?_ and Serena comes back with: _No!_

Comment

This exchange seems to be a transition between the second and third phase of the play. Silvia calls Serena back, despite their disagreements, and shows that she does want to continue to play with her. She calls Serena by name, and also indicates the role she attributes to her in the pretense: that of a help-mate. When she adds that if Serena doesn't come the baby will cry, she is using a valorizing strategy, probably because that gives her a better chance of persuading Serena to participate. And indeed, Serena immediately leaves Rocco and comes back to Silvia, thus showing that she is ready to continue to play with her.

Serena's first in-frame utterance, scolding the baby, does not help to establish a congenial atmosphere: Silvia is puzzled. Despite a conciliatory remark of Serena's and her getting water for the baby, Silvia remains hostile and makes a totally unexpected remark: _Why do you give him lemon?_ Sylvia marks up several points with this remark:

- To the glass Serena offers the baby she attributes a meaning that is in contradiction with what Serena herself had said.

- She asks for an explanation of this unjustly attributed meaning, thus creating a paradox for Serena, putting her into a double bind at the level of the direct meaning of the message. Her question is analogous to the well-known "When did you stop beating your wife?"

- She adds: *He doesn't want lemon,* indicating an attitude of power: I know what the baby needs, you don't, you're making a mistake.

Silvia seems to have found a way of keeping Serena in the pretend play by asking an apparently polite but paradoxical question that at the interpersonal level signals that Serena cannot have the role she would like to play. At this level, Silvia's question also creates a double-bind situation because she simultaneously expresses strong disagreement and a desire to continue shared play (which she had reaffirmed by saying that the baby would cry if Serena didn't come).

The intervention of a third person, Rocco, provides an opportunity to perhaps unravel the paradox. Serena uses Rocco's question *Why doesn't he want lemon?* to explain her attitude to Silvia. By answering: *She doesn't give him lemon, she gives him water,* Serena reverses roles, and attributes to Silvia the action of giving the baby something to drink. But she specifies that it was water, not lemon. Serena's answer to Rocco thus provides information at two different levels of communication:

- She provides Rocco with information about what is being given to the baby (water not lemon).
- She says that it is Silvia who is giving the baby something to drink, thus using the same procedure of wrong attribution that Silvia had used before.

Silvia does not seem to understand Serena's message. She takes it at face value and asks in surprise: *Is it water?* apparently accepting that the others ignored her wrong attribution (lemon, in contradiction to what Serena had said). Serena's *No!* in answer to Silvia's question *Is it water?* seems to confirm the double character of her previous utterance. Rather than contradicting the nature of what the baby is given to drink, she seems to deny that she is giving the baby something to drink. She appears to oppose the underlying meaning of Silvia's remarks (i.e., the put-down that Serena does not know how to take care of the baby). At this point, however, it is impossible for the children to clarify their misunderstanding based on false premises; they are not able to attribute the same values of agreement or disagreement to the propositions.

PHASE 3: ACTIVATION
OF SELF-CORRECTIVE MECHANISMS

During the third phase, the children reestablish their similarity or equality, they make the conflict explicit and manage the constraints that have to be accepted. The phase is composed of two parts:

(8) The two girls still want to play together.

(9) On neutral ground, the conflict can be made explicit.

8) Serena says to Silvia: *Why do you give him lemon?* Silvia cries: *Nooo!* and then starts to chant: *Lemon, lemon! Lemon, Simon! Lemon!, Lemon!* [In Italian, *limone* rhymes with *Simone*]. Rocco continues: *Lemon, lemon! My friend is called Simon! Lemon!* And Serena and Elisabeta join in: *Lemon, lemon!*

Comment

Serena addresses to Silvia the same paradoxical request for explanation that Silvia had addressed to her. It is Silvia's turn to be bewildered and to answer negatively. This exchange reproduces the same misunderstanding (as in 7), but with roles now reversed. Silvia's *No!* expresses neither agreement nor disagreement. She may have intended to say that it was to Serena that she had attributed the action of giving the baby lemon and not to herself; however that may be, the two girls are clearly at sixes and sevens. The paradoxical question may be considered to carry two meanings: On the one hand, it reestablishes some kind of similarity between the two, because Serena repeats Silvia's words, and places her in the same situation as she herself was before. On the other hand, the exchange of the two identities (I am now you, you are me) introduces an irrational element. Similarly, the premise (what I called water is lemon) violates the principle of noncontradiction. Such illogicalities can be tolerated within the context of pretense because in make-believe all transformations are possible. But at this point, Serena and Silvia have not yet clarified their relationship within the play or outside it; consequently what they say relates both to the theme of their play and to their interpersonal relationship. Emotionally, Serena's repetition of an utterance produced by Silvia signals a reestablishment of equality and an acceptance of Silvia herself. This is probably why Silvia joyfully reacts by inventing a song, in which all the children then join. Through the use of this ludic language a change takes place from the conflictual situation to a positively charged get-together where each is accepted by the other. The chanting together creates a relaxed feeling and emphasizes the children's desire to remain within a make-believe world. The word "lemon," which earlier was the object of discord, now gives rise to a rhyming pattern and leads to reconciliation. A symmetrical relation, positively charged in its affective meaning, is now established; but by itself it cannot lead to a solution of the problems that caused the deadlock (i.e., the difficulties of differentiation between self and others, reality and fiction, and make-believe and falsehood).

9) Serena goes down on all fours and barks like a dog: *Bow-wow!* Silvia reacts immediately: *Hello, little cat!* Rocco joins in: *Ow, wow!* Serena rectifies: *I am*

not a little cat, I am a dog!, and turning to Rocco, she says: *Come little cat–dog, I say bow-wow!* Rocco and Serena run along together on all fours, barking away. Then Serena goes toward Silvia, who was looking on and who now says to Serena: *Come little cat!* Once again Serena corrects her: *I am not the little cat!* But Silvia commands: *Say miaow!* Serena replies: *No, bow-wow!* and pretends to attack the doll (still on the chair). *No, he's little!* says Silvia, picking up the doll and running away to hide it. When she comes back she tries to wrest a spoon from Serena, saying: *The spoon!* Serena holds on and says: *No I won't give it to you!* Silvia then asks: *Will you do the little cat?* and Serena answers, running toward Rocco: *I don't know how, do it yourself!* Silvia once again calls Serena: *Are you coming?* But Serena chants: *I don't know how, no, no, no!*

Comment

A new theme is introduced, pretending to be animals, and this theme appears to provide an easier terrain for working out the conflict. Without having to deal with the difficult attribution of roles vis-à-vis the doll, it becomes possible to be clear about the real object of their disagreement, that is, the power of decision in the play. The dialogue concerning the cat and the dog seems to bring the conflict to the fore, so that both girls can become aware of its real nature. It may be easier for Serena to bring out her nonsubordination to Silvia when she is in a position to say that she is not a cat, but a dog. Emotionally, this assertion constitutes a step in the development of their conflict that previously was only implied (I disagree with you, but I cannot say it outright because I want to stay together with you). Now the verbal exchange clarifies their interpersonal relationship, and the incident of the spoon makes things even clearer. This nonsubordination reestablishes the principle of noncontradiction and of identity (if I am a dog I cannot be a cat); at the same time, Serena shows that when there is no conflict on the personal level, paradoxes are admissible in make-believe: speaking to Rocco, she calls him *little cat–dog*. Between Serena and Silvia the disagreement is now clear: *I can't do it, do it yourself!* says Serena. The two girls now appear to communicate on the same level and agree to disagree: They will reach a reciprocity that admits of differences.

PHASE 4: PRODUCTIVE NEGOTIATION AND RESUMPTION OF THE PRETENSE

The conflict will be resolved by joking.

10) Silvia continues: *Come here, little cat, the pap!* addressing Serena and laughing. Serena approaches Silvia, and once again barks like a dog. Silvia

remarks: *You're not the cat, eh? Serena, Serena, you're not the cat, eh? That's true!*
Serena answers: *But yes, I am the cat, bow-wow,* in a deep voice like a dog. Then
Serena sits down in the chair, facing Silvia. Silvia holds a glass out to Serena
who takes it and pretends to drink from it. She then gives it back to Silvia.
Silvia stands up for a moment, walks about, but comes back almost immediately and once again holds out the glass to Serena. Serena again pretends to
drink from the glass, hands it back and asks: *Is it orange juice?* Silvia takes the
glass back and answers: *No, it's not . . . it's not . . . it's pap!*

Comment

The pretend context is reestablished. Silvia once again proposes that Serena
should pretend to be a cat, but jokingly. She adds the "pap" idea, but now
without reference to the doll, and as soon as Serena says *bow-wow,* she declares that Serena is not a cat, and to make sure that her partner interprets
this utterance correctly, she insists: *That's true.* Silvia has clearly worked out
some problems pertaining to the distinction between make-believe and reality, and to the necessity of interpersonal agreement, at the level of pretend
play as well as at the level of their personal relations. Serena also has worked
out such problems: She can now accept being a cat, she can even affirm
her cat-ness in answer to Silvia's contrary suggestion and, accepting the role
of the cat, she barks like a dog. At this point, both girls have clearly entered
the world of pretense where it is even possible to be a cat–dog. Their utterances are felt by both to be pleasantries and are delivered laughingly. The
difference with the earlier phases is striking: The girls are no longer engaged
in serious reciprocal exploration and conflict. They are ready to start playing
together.

From this point on, Silvia accepts to play dinner without the doll, and they
play on for a long time without any confrontation. The two girls pretend to
feed each other, often asking questions such as: *Is that rice? Will you give me things
to eat?* The answer may be *No,* but is immediately followed by an explanation:
Not rice, pasta!

Possibly, the question-and-answer play concerning what the food consists
of is a symbolic transposition of the earlier confrontation about the pap, with
its underlying interpersonal conflict. This mode of communication continues
all along the cooperative episode (which lasts 20 minutes), and seems to show
that the girls, although aware of the possibility of conflict, are also aware that
conflict can be avoided and agreement confirmed. They seem to have taken
their distance from the initial discord, to have understood something about
the nature of their disagreements, and to have acquired strategies for sharpen-
ing conflict as well as for controlling it.

DISCUSSION: THE FOUR PHASES OF THE EPISODE
AND THEIR TRANSFORMATION

Phase 1: Initial Positioning, Exploration
of Zones of Tolerance and Ambiguity

The first phase of the episode illustrates the ambiguities that easily arise in make-believe and in the presence of several children, and shows how these ambiguities can lead to misunderstandings. This phase also illustrates that the possibilities for agreement and negotiation depend mainly on the first proposal of a theme and on the first exchanges between the partners.

The initial reciprocal positioning (i.e., the manner in which each partner enters into the play) is characterized by their first exchanges. Before negotiations can start, the partners each express their own interpretation of the pretend theme. Their first utterances determine, in a sense, the mode and development of the negotiations as well as the nature of the interpersonal relations. The beginning of the episode thus represents an exploration of each other's tolerance that will set limits to the possibilities of interaction. The exploration is closely linked to the first proposal of a theme and of roles; such proposals can be more or less general, more focused on a theme or more focused on roles. At our subjects' age, there is usually no explicit proposal for a pretense: The children are together in a group and often a proposal is expressed by an action that is then imitated by another child. Negotiations about roles and their distribution will depend on the relation between the first two children and the manner in which they may try to make other children join the play. Verbal proposals are often very general (e.g., Serena's *Dinner is ready!*) and are addressed to several children, who can interpret the invitation in their own way and decide whether to participate according to their own wishes. In the episodes analyzed, three main modes of positioning to the first proposals can be distinguished.

- Association and acceptance: some children by imitation join a child who initiated a pretend play or they immediately accept the roles and tasks the initiator assigns to them. In neither case is there a threat to the position of the initiator.

- Counterproposal: a child proposes something other than what the first child had proposed, although at the same time intimating agreement with the first one's idea of playing together. The initiating child then needs to reposition. If the counterproposal is compatible with the first, if it concerns a subtheme that does not threaten the positioning of the initiator, the negotiations will most likely bear on the distribution of roles and tasks within the main theme. If, however, the counterproposal leads to conflict (regarding both the pretend situation and the interpersonal relationship), an ambiguity may arise concerning which aspect of the interaction has to be negotiated: who decides the theme, or how the roles within the theme should be distributed. Counterproposals that cause conflict are often more attractive to the other children of the group and better structured, but generally also less open-ended than the initial proposal. In such cases (as illustrated by our example) it is difficult for the possible partners to come to an agreement, because it is necessary to start by clarifying on which level the negotiation is to take place.

- Incorporation: the new proposal does not contradict the first one, but reduces it to a subtheme. The author of the counterproposal claims the role of director, and the other child has to negotiate or submit.

In the case of counterproposals and incorporations, the negotiating process to a large extent depends on the strategy chosen by the second child. The first interactions between the partners are thus of primary importance for the definition of the level at which negotiation will take place. The various values of the messages that are given (acceptance, refusal, denial) are often not immediately clear.

In the example given, Silvia immediately makes a (nonverbal) counterproposal to Serena. Serena tries to incorporate this counterproposal without changing her position as the initiator, but she does not define a wider play context within which Silvia might negotiate her positioning. As a result, the level of negotiation is unclear and both girls feel frustrated. At the level of choosing the leader in the play, Serena feels threatened; at the level of content, Silvia is frustrated. The level of negotiation is consequently ambiguous right from the start. In fact, what the girls engage in may be called pseudonegotiations: Neither is aware of the ambiguity and each adopts strategies aiming at continuing shared play without relinquishing her own initiative.

Strategies of persuasion and concession may be refused or countered. Each girl tries unsuccessfully to persuade her partner as if the partner were willing to change; concessions are made only for the purpose of staying together, without any suggestion being made of changing the contrasting projects. The girls' attitudes lead to the adoption of strategies that are alternately directed to self-affirmation (by direct opposition or by devalorization of the other) and to the recovery of agreement with the other (through various concessions).

These alternating strategies (centered on the self or on the other) seem to arise from certain presuppositions regarding the partner that may be denied or countered by similar presuppositions held by the latter. Strategies of devalorization or denial of the other are often manifested by treating the partner as a passive object (e.g., by taking a toy away from her) or as nonexistent (e.g., by answering a question in her place). Such behavior creates perplexity in the partner or leads her to redefine herself (I brought this doll along; *I* should do this). Recognition or acceptance of the other leads to concessions, which may also be based on arbitrary presuppositions. Various strategies of seduction, justification, and reformulation of projects were observed, but although these strategies were aimed at reestablishing recognition of the other, they usually did not make the object of the conflict explicit. Sometimes one of the partners renounced her own project and adhered for a moment to the other's idea, but, as soon as agreement was reached, she reverted to her own plan.

A frequent presupposition consists in the idea that as soon as the partner joins again in the play, it is admissible to return to one's own project as if the problem were solved. Indeed, the agreement usually remains operative on the level of continuing the play, but the other's interpretation of the agreement may be based on a different presupposition.

Such sequences of presuppositions and alternating strategies are dependent on the partners' ability to distinguish the different levels of communication, which is particularly difficult in pretend play. Often the double meanings of messages lead to misunderstandings: There is disagreement, but each partner thinks the other agrees, and when the disagreement comes out into the open, each thinks that it is she herself who is not accepted by the other. Two frequent strategies (i.e., the implicit restructuration of the scenario and the arbitrary attribution of an intention to the partner) aim at persuading the partner to change roles or to accept an imposed role. These strategies are applied by one of the partners while appearing to continue playing as before (by presupposing that the other agrees on the distribution of the roles in the pretense and/or on the role of the leader).

If the conflict is not interpersonal and if the proposed theme or role is an interesting alternative, such strategies may lead to an immediate coordination that, according to Giffin (1984, p. 91), allows the introduction of transformations within the development of the pretense. But when, as in the example given, the direct relationship between the children is ambiguous or conflictual, and when an agreement presupposed by one is contradicted by the other, the children will continue their interpersonal explorations, agreements will prove transitory, renunciations are not genuine, the conflict is not really understood, and the children remain dissatisfied.

Nonetheless, the variety and coherent sequence of the various strategies attest to the children's sensitivity to the other's reactions because each refusal is followed by a change in behavior aimed at reaching agreement. The children also show a tendency to conserve earlier propositions because each agreement is followed by a return to the initial project. The indirect persuasion strategies, even when they fail to convince the other, attest to the children's cognitive capacity of continuing a plan without displeasing the other and without facing internal conflict. The first part of the example illustrates this capacity by its sequence of acceptance and refusal, affirmation of one's own project, and incorporation of the other's.

The fact that the children seem astonished when their partner does not agree and that they ask for explanations corroborates the hypothesis that they presuppose the existence of an agreement. The ambiguity concerning Silvia's utterance *The pap* disturbs the positive affective climate because it obscures the real nature of the discord. Both girls are irritated; they feel intuitively that the rules of communication have been violated and Serena departs (3) as if aware that something has to be changed for a new solution to become possible.

Phase 2: Retroactive Control Processes

Retroactive control processes are procedures by which subjects acquire insight into the way their interaction has developed and the use they make of this insight for the introduction of changes in their further interaction. Whenever the strategies they adopt prove unsuitable and an unforeseen result ensues, they feel the need to change the result or at least to understand it better.

In the example given, Serena's irritation and her departure mark the beginning of a crisis in which the self–other rule is invalidated and the limits of the reciprocity presupposition have to be redefined through a focus on the internal constraints of each person.

The first step is a repetition of the strategies that were already used (i.e., another attempt by Serena to restructure the scenario and to eliminate the doll; *He doesn't want to swallow*). Serena proceeds to check if there was indeed some tacit agreement (because Silvia accepted the pot she gave her), and finds that Silvia clearly disagrees. Serena's repetition of the persuasion strategies she used in the first phase fails, and it becomes evident that Silvia does not want to change the pretend theme. As before, Silvia does accept collaboration, but no direct activity with the doll on Serena's part. Serena repeats a strategy of concession, when she protects Silvia against Rocco's intrusion and helps her to feed the doll. The limits of their interpersonal tolerance have been redefined, but their interaction, as in the first phase, is still a pseudonegotiation. Sometimes the control process stops at this point, and the pseudonegotiation continues with an endless series of persuasion and concession strategies (marginal to the conflict) and a few harmonious sequences (also marginal to the conflict). The dissatisfied partner always comes back to the initial request as if possibly something had changed in the meantime.

The second step consists in the establishment of an internal balance sheet of the situation, leading to a radical revision of interpersonal attitudes. This step is illustrated by Serena's reaction to Rocco's intervention and her leaving the play, without explanation. The fact that she immediately returns when Silvia calls asking her to help with the baby (signaling a change of attitude) seems to indicate that Serena indeed was thinking about what went on before, evaluating the situation.

Serena's departure is, for Silvia, an unexpected event that triggers the same process. Until then, Silvia had adopted an attitude of total concentration on her project, but she shows her capacity of recovering all the information that will allow her to persuade Serena to come back. She not only emphasizes the role Serena had already agreed to play: *Come and help me with the baby*, but she even adds: *Or . . . he's going to cry!* showing that she has perfectly understood why Serena is unhappy. This constitutes a new proposal. Silvia's behavior illustrates the complexity of the retroactive control process, which recovers the underlying meanings of the preceding exchanges and makes it possible to express what has not yet been said.

This resumption of the situation puts it on a different basis. In what follows, the partners make it clear that they have changed their system of possible choices. As was already pointed out, during pseudonegotiations many persuasion and concession strategies appear, but always according to the rule of alternating between self and other, with each partner remaining focused on her own project. At first, the partners are not aware of their own internal complexities (their double-edged desire not to displease the other but neither to renounce their own project) nor of the other's complexities. Both their inter- and intrapersonal perception is erroneous: It simplifies matters and leads to pseudoagreements and pseudodisagreements. When the system is changed, the clear expression of refusals represents an empirical proof that earlier premises have to be modified. In the example, the girls reach a kind of radicalization of their positions; they seem to have assimilated the rule of an alternation between self and other by the application of a control process on what went on before, and rejecting this rule, they choose one of the poles: either self or the other. At this point, renunciation (formerly always avoided) becomes an option: Serena goes away, and Silvia calls her back. The partners no longer think that the other can easily be manipulated, and they discover that manipulation can result in strong opposition that has to be taken into account. This awareness may lead the partners to forget their own inner complexity (i.e., their desire to continue communal play as well as to retain their own role as the leader).

Following renunciation it becomes clear that interpersonal negotiation has to be pursued further in order to attain an inner integration of self and other. In this phase, Serena's renunciation and Silvia's concession, both opted for as a choice between all and none, are still as fragile as the alternation between persuasion and concession in the former system: In a sense, both children are back where they started.

This phase also highlights the importance of expressing internal constraints during interpersonal exploration while productive negotiations are not yet possible. The crisis triggered by Silvia's paradoxical injunction, leading to a communication block, will incite the girls to take the next step.

Phase 3: Self-Corrective Mechanisms
Within the Interactional System

Self-corrective mechanisms in the interactional system serve the purpose of reestablishing the conditions for communication. The retroactive processes are affective as well as cognitive: They imply that each partner recognizes violations of interpersonal reciprocity (valorization and devalorization of the other as a person) and violations of the rules of rational dialogue (attributing the same meaning to agreement as to disagreement). Because the children stop acting and try to change something, they must presuppose a rule whose violations they repudiate. This does not mean, however, that they are conscious of the rule, nor that they can discuss its violations rationally. Nonetheless, their sensitivity to the other's reactions and their empathy set the corrective mechanisms in motion, so that the wrong presuppositions of the one are refuted by the other and gradually corrected. Each exchange becomes a source of information about the other's functioning as well as a means of regulating one's own behavior; thus an intrapersonal exploration is brought about that favors a better insight into one's own complexities. In the case of Silvia and Serena, the process is complicated by the pretend situation, which encourages ambiguities that are all the more difficult to unravel because the children have to deal with the opacity of spoken language, with the problem of the differentiation and integration of self and other, as well as with the distinction between fiction and reality. At the conclusion of this phase, the children are thus confronted with a crisis: Communication is blocked.

When a communication block is the result of a lengthy reciprocal exploration, the children rarely become discouraged. They are ready to leave behind whatever triggered the block and to concentrate on understanding what led to it. They clearly consider their interdependence as a precondition for all further activity. They show each other that they are ready to accept the crisis as a crisis and to deal with it, although the situation may strike the observer as a deviation from the aims they were pursuing before.

This readiness of children to squarely confront difficult situations needs emphasis because it shows that they have an early representation of the social world that is very different from what is often supposed. Adults usually try to avoid situations that are difficult for children and to reinforce their capacity for occulting internal conflicts rather than to let them bring the difficulties into the open and to overcome them. The interpersonal negotiations between Serena and Silvia show that exposing the conflicts may provide information crucial for an escape from a precarious system of alternatives that suffers from many errors of interpersonal perception. The abandonment of the pretend play, the explicit refusals and the shared discovery of internal conflicts can be an invaluable experience for learning to overcome intra- and interpersonal disequilibria and to search for the reciprocity which is indispensable for genuine agreement.

As Wallon (cf. 1949, pp. 103–108) often claimed, such functional adaptation is a characteristic of all human beings who need interdependence both for survival and for the exploration of the external world. This universal need for interdependence makes it possible for children as well as adults to confront and overcome paradoxical situations through interaction.

During this phase, five instances may be distinguished when self-corrective mechanisms redress the violations that led to the communication block.

1. The violations are recognized; the children change their strategies, the level of their communications, and their interpersonal attitudes.

2. A counterparadox is used in order to reestablish a similarity between self and other.

3. This similarity is used in order to consolidate rules that were already acquired: ludic language.

4. The rules are used in order to further the process of differentiation between self and other: the dog–cat invention.

5. The differentiation between self and other is used in order to further the integration of self and other: I don't know how to do it, but you do.

This last step toward direct communication indicates the construction of a new rule as an alternative to the earlier system that was founded on the polarization of self and other. Serena can now once again choose renunciation, but this time without devalorizing Silvia. On the contrary, she now recognizes Silvia as a person and accepts the limitations of her possible role within the situation proposed by Silvia. Serena's progress took place from an alternation between self and other (the use of indirect strategies to bring about changes in the other) to a polarization of self and other (renunciation of the play and of the other) and, finally, to an integration between self and other (renunciation of the play, but conservation of communication by means of a clarification of her incapacity to comply).

The counterparadox (*Why do you give him lemon?*) can be considered as a positive as well as a negative retroaction because it simultaneously implies the impossibility of rational communication and an unconditional interpersonal acceptance that allows Silvia to invent a reassuring situation. The ludic intermezzo of the communal chant acts as an emotional stabilizer but also as a transition to a clearer mode of verbal communication: the cat–dog sequence. This sequence can be interpreted as a metaphor that allows the real problem (i.e., the relation between yes and no in make-believe and in reality) to be defined. The children's exchanges at this point are neither rational nor purely ludic, but they lead to rational communication and to a retake of the pretense: the conflict is resolved (you're not the cat—Yes, I am the cat) and the reciprocity and distribution of roles are consolidated. Similar strategies are used by adults (cf. Watzlawick et al., 1967). From a different point of view, Wallon (1949, p. 107) considered that emotional contagion and ritual provide for the transition from emotion toward rationality in the history of the human species. Fonzi and Negro-Sanzipriano (1975) stressed the role of metaphors and considered this mode of communication a form of cognitive comprehension of the many contradictory aspects of reality that are difficult to analyze by deductive thinking.

The children in our example are not yet able to metacommunicate about the conflict and have not yet achieved a differentiation between self and other that would allow them to prevent conflicts and to negotiate efficiently; but they do possess the resources to enter into productive negotiations. Peer interaction seems to provide especially favorable opportunities for the exteriorization of these resources and for the invention of rules that allow for progress both in the construction of the self and in the development of communicative competence.

Phase 4: Productive Negotiation

The necessary conditions for fruitful negotiation can be summed up as follows:

1. In order to open negotiations, premises have to be shared that ensure reciprocity of interdependence. This reciprocity may be called in question by strategies that appear to ignore the other (e.g., answer in the other's place, communicate via a third person, etc.).

2. To develop negotiations fruitfully, the negotiators have to be clear about the object, they have to discuss the same problem. If there is doubt about the object of the negotiation, misunderstandings may arise.

3. In order to reach a satisfactory result, alternatives have to be proposed concerning the problem in hand as well as the internal constraints of the interpersonal relationship: Eventual renunciation has to be evaluated according to one's own satisfaction or dissatisfaction, and persuasion according to the internal constraints of the other. Productive negotiation thus implies an equilibrium between the efficacy of persuasion and one's own satisfaction within a context of interdependence that is understood by both, and experienced as an internal conflict as well as a conflict between self and other.

Productive negotiation leads either to renunciation (but without devalorization of the other, and without a break in the interpersonal communication so that each still disposes of possibilities for moves), or to an agreement that integrates the desires of both, due to a reciprocally satisfying combination of persuasion and concession. In both cases individual renunciations take place that imply an internal dialogue of the parties to a conflict. In Wallon's (1949) developmental theory, this corresponds to the time when the other in relation to the self ceases to be situated in the particular person on whom the child has crystallized one of the polarities, and becomes an abstract interlocutor, a partner in an internal dialogue.

Various communicative strategies are used by the children and an analysis of the many episodes observed led to distinguishing the following categories:

- Integration of self and other: discovery and management of internal constraints (e.g., I am not able to do this, you do it; or: I do it like this, how do you do it?).
- Use of temporal order (e.g., first I, then you).
- Simultaneous use of yes and no in pretend play (e.g., You're the cat . . . you're not the cat).
- Use of spatial relations (e.g., I brought this along, we'll put it between us).

The use of these strategies shows that the children are able to construct utterances that include both I and another, that express spatiotemporal relations and that, in the context of a pretend play, combine yes and no. In the example reported here, Serena arrives at a construction of personal capacity (I can—I cannot) by a limitation of her ego in contrast with her feeling of total power (real or presumed) that underlay the initial pseudonegotiation.

CONCLUDING REMARKS

For 3-year-old children, the processes that lead to the reciprocal acceptance of self and other are complex and resemble, as to their mechanisms, the interpersonal negotiations that have been studied within the family (parents, children, couples). Silvia's paradoxical strategy or the subtle shift between pretense and cheating performed by Serena when she wants her partner to abandon her project with the doll confuse the adult observer as well as the children. As adults, we also suffer from ambiguous communication and the difficulty of deciding whether a message carries the meaning of an agreement or a refusal. It is often difficult to find our way out of a blind alley and the communication blocks we encounter are similar to those experienced by children: Often we no longer know what we are talking about, who said what, or why an agreement that seemed to be solid is suddenly put in question by behavior that is felt to be a denial of evidence, a denial of one's self and of one's relationship with the other. As adults, we then wonder about the history of the relationship, about our own capacity for understanding, our sensitivity and the strategies that led to a transformation of (pseudo-)agreements into far-reaching discord. We may be afraid to delve more deeply into interpersonal exploration, maybe because we do not want to risk a refusal or an internal conflict.

Serena and Silvia, and other children in other episodes, show that they do not hesitate to run the risk of a break and of discovering their own internal conflicts. They follow a primary social principle: It is impossible to avoid human interdependence, it is necessary to interact with others. They manage to construct strategies that open the way to a new way of interacting. In their relations, the children use, so to say, a mode of functioning that is founded on similarity between them. At first, they position themselves as if the other were able to understand their contradictory desires (I desire to do what I want, but I also want to stay with you). Later, they are able to change their attitude: Confronted with a refusal, they activate spontaneous self-correcting mechanisms. The awareness of similarity between human beings can be a facilitating factor in social interaction. One aspect of the similarity is particularly important: People's reactions cannot always be foreseen. When children realize this, they learn to enrich their inventory of strategies in order to reestablish contact.

The many negotiation sequences observed in the various videotapes, show the children's willingness to change their attitudes according to their partners' reactions. At first, these modifications consist in a strategy of alternation between valorization of the other and valorization of a personal project. This strategy does not always succeed but leads to interpersonal adjustments. The children are able to conserve what is achieved by the dynamics of their interaction, as it is founded on a reciprocal recognition of each other as persons. In our view, this process contributes to the psychological differentiation between self and other.

ACKNOWLEDGMENTS

I am grateful to the children of the day-care center San Gottardo, Comune di Genoa, for their inventive play and to the staff of the center for their valuable collaboration.

Chapter 4

Psychosocial Knowledge as Reflected in Puppet Shows Improvised by Pairs of Children*

Sylvie Rayna
Monique Ballion
Monique Bréauté
Mira Stambak
Institut National de Recherche Pédagogique, Paris

This study of psychosocial knowledge among children was undertaken in a kindergarten that accepts children from ages 2 to 4. Among other activities, the children have the option of performing puppet shows—a very special kind of pretend play—in a room equipped for the purpose.

To improvise a puppet show that will hold the attention of an audience composed of adults and of children of the same age as the puppeteers is a task bound by precise social rules and differs strikingly from "free" pretend play. In a puppet show, there is no lack of creative freedom, but it is a freedom limited by the constraints of the medium.

Because a kind of kindergarten rule was adopted that there should always be two children to work the puppets, the shows take on the character of shared pretend play.

So far we have studied the young puppeteers' communicative, cognitive, and theatrical capabilities (Bréauté et al., 1987; Stambak, Ballion, Bréauté & Rayna, 1985; Stambak & Royon, 1985). Shared improvisation with puppets also sheds light on the players' social world and we agree with authors for whom pretend play, and especially pretend play among several children, favors the development of social knowledge, as first suggested by Mead (1934).

How do the children go about inventing a play for two? How far can they adjust one to the other? How do they come to agree on a theme they will act

---

*This chapter is based on observations made in Paris.

out together? Do they show knowledge of human reactions and how these reactions may influence the behavior of others?

Within the play, what are the relations between the characters portrayed? Is it possible to discern what conception the children have of interpersonal relations between adults and children, and of adults and children amongst themselves?

These are some of the questions we attempt to answer in this chapter.

THEORETICAL FRAMEWORK

This study is part of a series undertaken by Centre de Recherche de l'Education Spécialisée et de l'Adaptation Scolaire—Institut National de Recherche Pédagogique (CRESAS-INRP) in schools and preschool centers under the general heading of social interaction and the construction of knowledge (CRE-SAS, 1987). More particularly, the various researches relate to the facts that in France academic failure is massive and socially selective (i.e., it occurs mostly among children from lower social strata). Work carried on during some 15 years has gradually convinced us that such failure is preventable (CRESAS, 1981).

From our point of view, every child wants to learn and can acquire knowledge, including what is prescribed in school programs. We thus share the aims of those who are working for increased academic success. We believe this goal to be attainable, but only if educational practice is based on how the individual actually acquires and extends knowledge.

Research carried out from day-care center to primary school brought us to adopt a constructivist approach toward understanding the learning process (Sinclair et al., 1982/1989). This means repudiating the idea that knowledge is a possession transmissible to another person as if it were an object. From the constructivist point of view, which we derive from Piaget and Wallon, children from birth pursue exploratory activities constantly querying and testing the real world. All knowledge accordingly is built up gradually; what is acquired will need to be reconstructed; and each discovery raises new questions.

Pursuing our research, we gradually became convinced of the primary importance of social interactions and of the need to integrate them in the constructivist perspective (Stambak et al., 1983; Stambak & Verba, 1986; Verba, Stambak, & Sinclair, 1982). Concepts such as exchanges, cooperation, and confrontation were included in our approach. Interaction between partners (adult–child, child–child) favors not only the mobilization of already acquired knowledge but also the construction of new knowledge (Stambak, 1988). What happens from our point of view is a co-construction of knowledge.

In this study, children's psychosocial knowledge was viewed during an activity that suits our theoretical framework. The fact that there are two children to work the puppets leads them to create the show jointly in constant interaction. Because the show is a kind of pretend play, interaction is manifest on two levels: (a) between partners in the build-up and development of their scenes; (b) between the various characters represented by the puppets.

Method

Our work is pursued in educational establishments via action research, the main feature of which is the setting up of close collaboration between the researchers and the educational practitioners (day-care staff, teachers, etc.) so that research becomes a joint venture. This is a lengthy process with regular in-depth discussions concerning joint experiments in specially arranged educational situations that are evaluated on the basis of the children's behavior. The process, which we call *regulatory autoevaluation*, allows the team of researchers and practitioners to co-construct new knowledge about children and about educational practice.

In this context, the creation of a puppet workshop in the kindergarten was proposed. It needs to be explained that the proposal was not made by the researchers out of the blue, for the staff, on the initiative of the head of the kindergarten, had already been giving puppet shows for all the children as well as for smaller groups in order to introduce the children to certain activities (Bréauté et al., 1987). The puppet project grew out of initiatives and successive attempts by each of the staff members and out of their discussions with the researchers.

How does the project work? A small puppet theater (like for a Punch-and-Judy show) is provided for the children's use as one of the activities proposed at the start of the day. The theater box is placed on a carpet and the puppets are of the kind where one inserts one's hand in the puppet's cloth garment (little girl, little boy, big dog, etc.). The children who decide to join the project are free to be either members of the audience or puppeteers. Making a list of who gets a turn poses no problem. Two children who want to put on a show kneel behind the theater (the tops of their bodies remain visible) and straightaway launch into their improvisation in front of the other children.

Recording and Analysis of Data

Over 2 school years, we made videotapes of pairs of children, ages 2 to 4 engaged in improvisational puppet shows. These are natural observations in the sense that the shows were filmed as part of the normal activities of the kindergarten.

The tapes were transcribed with the help of the teachers; not only were the children's actions and utterances noted exhaustively, but also their facial expressions, their gestures, and the way they manipulate the puppets. The reactions of the audience were also noted, especially if they were verbal.

Our analysis of the puppet plays showed that they were composed of several acts, each consisting either in a scene with a storyline or in what we called a "musical" (i.e., a combination of singing and dancing). It proved easy to identify these scenes because each forms a coherent whole and consists in the definition of a theme, its development, and, at the end, a kind of conclusion. Changing to a new scene is generally marked by the introduction of a new theme and often goes together with a change in the puppets the children manipulate. Sometimes there is continuity between scenes: in that case, the puppet play is equivalent to a set of variations on the same theme.

In this chapter, our special interest is in the children's psychosocial knowledge. Puppet plays produced by seven pairs of children are presented. Six pairs of children were essentially of the same age; in one pair, there was an age difference of 8 months:

Marie (3;0) and Julie (3:0)

Charlotte (3;4) and Alexandra (3;3)

Diane (3;4) and Noëline (3;2)

Noëline (3;2) and Elisa (3;3)

Thomas (3;6) and Yohanna (3;4)

Clément (3;8) and Alexandre (4;1)

Maria (3;6) and Stéphane (2;10).

The following analyses were carried out. First, like the other contributors to this volume, we were interested in negotiations between the children, in particular the negotiations that take place between two partners while they are deciding on the theme that is to be developed. The interactive processes operative in this phase of mutual adjustment bear witness to the children's ability to collaborate with peers.

Second, the children develop original little stories of dramatic interest, staging well-defined characters having their own interpersonal relations. An analysis of these relations provides entry into the children's representations of the social world they inhabit.

Third, the final section of this chapter is concerned with the part played by the children's considerable theatrical know-how in objectivizing their psychosocial knowledge.

ABILITY FOR INTERACTION
IN NEGOTIATING PLAY THEMES

In the seven puppet plays presented, all the scenes were constructed by the two partners, which implies that they had to agree on a theme. We try to show that to reach agreement it is necessary to interact efficiently with one's partner and to establish a relationship that allows the resolution of eventual sociocognitive conflicts; we will also try to shed some light on the kind of psychosocial knowledge that underlies the capacity for mutual adjustment.

Many authors who have studied collective pretense are interested in this aspect of children's play. Garvey and Berndt (1977), Giffin (1984), and Stockinger-Forys and McCune-Nicolich (1984) have all published studies on how children come to agree on the make-believe character of play, and how they manage to construct shared systems of meaning. These authors analyzed not only the children's exchanges during pretend play, but also the procedures used in choosing a theme, the distribution of parts and the symbolic transformation of objects used as props. They agree that for collective pretend play the children need to possess communicative skills as well as shared social representations. Forbes et al. (1986) presented a detailed analysis of setting up a pretense in their study of pretend play in 5-year olds. He and his collaborators showed that certain theme proposals are met by refusal or resistance and that in the subsequent negotiations interpersonal persuasion plays a large part. According to these authors, the main reason for accepting or refusing a proposal is the need to maintain a coherent framework for the play.

These studies were mainly based on the observation of free pretend play, and we share their authors' points of view. Our study, by contrast, concerns a particular situation with its specific constraints: The children have to produce puppet shows for other children of the kindergarten, and this socially defined task implies that the audience has to be kept interested. Furthermore, the puppeteers are clearly expected to portray fictional events, and they know this very well. They can thus immediately start by choosing their puppets, making them act, and speaking for them. As soon as two children have taken up some puppets, their agreement to perform a play is clearly observable: They look at one another, explain why they chose the particular puppets, and smile. The next task is to decide on a theme they will develop for the audience.

In our observations, the children agree surprisingly quickly about a theme, at the very beginning of their play as well as at the start of a new scene. At their age, our subjects do not yet prepare their performance as older children would; they do not announce the content of the scenes beforehand, but they improvise, and their first exchanges lead them to an idea that can be developed in the play. Sometimes the agreement is immediate, and sometimes there is brief negotiation. Examples of both follow.

Immediate Agreement

Thomas (3;6) chooses Big Dog and puts him in an attack position toward Little Girl chosen by Yohanna (3;4); Big Dog then bites Little Girl. Yohanna immediately accepts the proposal of the nasty dog theme: She mimes the fear of Little Girl by making her go backward. Thomas and Yohanna's entire puppet play develops around this theme (the example is reported in detail, in the section in which the children's ideas about relations between people and animals are discussed).

Marie (3;0) and Julie (3;0) have been acting as puppeteers in several scenes. Marie proposes a new theme: holding Man and Little Girl she brings them toward Julie, who is taking up Little Boy and Policeman. Marie says: *We're cold, we're cold!* Julie immediately enters into this new make-believe: *Me too I'm cold, I'm cold!* and she shivers. A new scene starts and the children have the puppets discuss the clothes one has to put on when it rains, and so forth.

Sometimes the audience contributes to the choice of theme. Noëline (3;2) and Diane (3;4) start a new play. Noëline has taken up Bird, holds it toward the audience and cries: *Who stole my cake?* One of the children in the audience answers, pointing to the Grandmother puppet in Diane's hand: *Granny did!* Diane shows that she accepts the idea that Granny is guilty by making her pick up a tin (the cake) and putting it in front of Noëline. The next scene to develop from this beginning centers on the idea of teasing.

Consultations With a View to Agreement

In most cases, however, agreement on what theme to develop is not as immediate, and the children need to exchange several remarks before a decision is reached. In some cases, one of the children shows a total lack of comprehension of the partner's intentions or proposals, whereupon the partner needs to clarify or explain. In other cases, it is clear that the children's intentions regarding the theme diverge, whereupon both try to defend or impose their original idea until one of them gives in. This entails genuine negotiation.

Strategies Leading to Mutual Understanding

It may be stated at once that it is rare for the children not to understand each other's rejoinder. Some examples have been encountered in the development of a scene (Stambak & Royon, 1985), but in the phase of seeking agreement on a theme it is quite exceptional.

When in the course of a show a proposal is suddenly made to change the theme, the partner may be baffled. This happens in the play put on by Noëline (3;2) and Elisa (3;3). In the middle of the show, Noëline unexpectedly proposes a new theme by addressing Elisa: *O Daddy, say, will you please buy some candy!* just when Elisa had taken up Little Bear. Disconcerted, Elisa shows her surprise and asks: *What happened?* Noëline thereupon picks up her theme in a different way: *Candy, Daddy, candy.* This time Elisa understands and adopts the suggested new role of the indulgent father. It will be noted that Noëline grasps her partner's incomprehension and proceeds to clarification by repeating her idea simplified to the bare essentials.

The active search for mutual comprehension is further illustrated in a show put on by two children of relatively different age: Maria (3;6) and Stéphane (2;10). These two children are not equal in theatrical competence. It is our observation that children from age 3 are able to develop a scenario. The younger children—2 to 3 years—are capable of producing characters and have ideas about animating the puppets, but their ideas do not really lead to further development.

In the analysis of Maria and Stéphane's show it appears quite clearly that Maria, the older child, gradually realizes that it is not possible to develop ideas with the younger one in the same way as with a child her own age. It is not that Stéphane does not want to do the show—the initial agreement is clearly expressed by an affectionate gesture between two puppets—but he has trouble adjusting to Maria's proposals. Faced with Stéphane's difficulty, Maria tries various strategies to get a show going between the two of them.

The first themes suggested by Maria are not followed up: At the outset, Maria, who has taken up Clown, puts forward an idea: *Bye bye, off to work I am.* But Stéphane fails to pick up the cue: *Me I've got Fido,* he says. So Maria tries another tack. She picks up Goblin, presents the puppet to Stéphane and proposes: *But, my papa sings, the little goblin talks, the little goblin talks.* This time Stéphane replies: *My papa say no goblin to me.* Then, holding Big Dog, he says: *Bow-wow!*

Obviously Stéphane is not taking up Maria's suggestions. The disagreement he evinces is probably linked to his lack of understanding (an attitude that will be encountered several times) and may depend on any of the following:

- Stéphane has a different conception of the task in hand and does not realize the urgency of picking up a theme and getting the show going. Like the younger children he is happy to present and animate some puppet character.

- He has difficulty with the complexities of Maria's proposal and with the way she formulates it.

- He experiences additional difficulty in entering the theatrical conventions. Maria's utterance . . . *my papa sings* . . . is not interpreted as the point of departure for a scenario but as an encouragement for him to relate something from his personal experience.

So Maria tries to help him. He hurried to pick up Goblin and is trying in vain to get his hand into the puppet. Maria takes it from him and tries to show him how to do it: *Hold on . . . I'll help you . . . you put your finger like that . . .* Stéphane refuses her assistance and prefers to take hold of Little Girl, a puppet that is easier to get onto one's hand. Maria, who during this brief episode realized that it was difficult for Stéphane to gear into her proposals, now also realizes that he has difficulty in manipulating the puppets. He's a little guy, so one has to come down to his level, she seems to be saying to herself. Maria accordingly tries to get the show going by starting from an idea of Stéphane's, whereas he picks up part of the theme suggested at the outset by Maria.

Stéphane brings Little Girl close to Goblin (still held by Maria), says: *Avar!* (uninterpreted) and quickly dips Little Girl down in front of the theater only to lift her up again with his arm stretched out. He is playing the game of appearance and disappearance that children frequently use as a kind of tease. Maria immediately gears in by having Goblin bend over the front of the theater saying: *I don't see anybody there!* Stéphane replies at once: *There, he's gone, there, there!* and once again waves Little Girl in the air. In these exchanges the children seem to be attempting to put themselves on the same footing.

Maria then tries to introduce a new idea taking into account that Stéphane apparently wants the puppets to play silly tricks. She activates Big Dog: *Look, he's again eating flour,* and putting a building block into the puppet's mouth she says: *You see it? He swallowed the flour.* But Stéphane, still immersed in his game of peekaboo, takes hold of the block, lifts it up in the air, and then puts it into the hand of his puppet: *There he is.* Maria understands that Stéphane is not participating in her new proposal and that he will not be able to continue the new theme.

She suggests to Stéphane what he should say: *You say, Fido, Fido has eaten the t'ing.* Stéphane does not repeat the suggested line, but does enter into Maria's idea because he has Little Girl lift up Big Dog and then hits Big Dog, doling out to him the expected punishment. Maria then also hits Big Dog with her puppet. Seeing that the theme foolery-punishment appeals to her young partner, Maria gets him to play at two educators reacting to a naughty dog, who here symbolizes a child. From this point on, the partners succeed in developing together a number of other highly amusing scenes one of which is analyzed later.

So the older child had to find out what theme the younger one would like to develop; hence the initial period of trial and error. At no time did Maria show any signs of impatience or fatigue. On the contrary, she was seen to deploy a variety of strategies to get her partner to agree to a theme. Sometimes she tried "tutoring," guiding him or telling him what to do, and for this type of intervention she needed to step out of the scenario frame and address him as a co-producer. She quickly understood that this strategy was not effective: Stéphane refused her assistance and did not follow her suggestions. It is only when she accepted his proposal, or rather when she carried forward an idea emanating from him that the two succeeded in producing coherent scenes that captured the attention of the public.

It thus appears that when the partners do not possess equivalent theatrical abilities, reciprocal adjustment takes more time. To settle on a scenario there is then need for a longer period of negotiation beset with refusals and instances of incomprehension that sometimes are hard to disentangle. It seems to us that when it comes to knowledge of other people, Maria clearly realizes that in theatrical ability there is a gap between her and Stéphane. Via the difficulties she encounters to make herself understood and the obstacles she has to overcome, Maria builds up her knowledge of the understanding and capacity for adaptation of children younger than herself. There is of course a twofold learning process, for in addition to Maria's progressive understanding of her partner's limitations there is Stéphane who is learning how to develop a coherent scene.

Persuasion Strategies in Negotiation

When two children's intentions diverge, what strategies might be employed to have one's idea accepted? An interesting example is provided by Marie (3;0) and Julie (3;0) who, in their lengthy show in the course of different scenes, manage to persuade each other to switch themes without offense to either partner.

At one point in the show, Julie wants to take up again a "devouring" scene they had played before, but Marie does not agree. While Julie advances Man toward Big Dog saying: *Go get it!* as if offering the dog some food, Marie pulls back Big Dog saying: *Wait!*. Julie repeats in a louder voice: *Go!* and offers Man to Big Dog. Marie in coaxing tones says: *Wait, will you wait*, and then introduces her new idea: *Fido has done poo-poo?* which Julie immediately accepts. Together they then act out a scene on this new theme.

In order to have her way and change the theme, Marie uses a dilatory tactic that keeps Julie in suspense and allows Marie to find a new idea that is satisfactory to both.

A little later in their show, Marie puts forward another idea: *I'll put Fido to bed.* Julie would prefer to continue with the theme just mentioned: *There he's done poo . . . he's peed in his bed!* But Marie who wants to play at being the adult looking after a baby says: *No, no, wait. I'll put a nappy on him.* Marie goes on to comment each of her actions with Julie looking on. For the time being, Julie gives up her idea and adopts Marie's. So when Marie says that the baby is asleep, Julie continues by proposing that some food should be prepared without waking the baby. Marie agrees and then suggests that the baby is waking up. Julie at once picks up her idea again of punishment for misbehavior, although remaining within the frame of the waking baby, and Marie agrees to play the scolding adult.

This time it was Julie who used compromise to achieve acceptance of her initially refused proposal: She starts by accepting her partner's theme and at the right moment reformulates her own proposal. After the concession that respects her partner's wishes, Julie's suggestion is accepted.

To quote another example: Charlotte (3;4), in a brilliant sequence, uses a variety of means to get Alexandra (3;3) to accept her idea. She wants to convince Alexandra to change puppets, to abandon Big Dog in favor of Little Girl.

She starts by several times calling out to Little Girl: *Sophie! Sophie!* then, brandishing her puppet Little Boy, she explains: *I wanna, I want speak with her*, and again quite emphatically: *I want to speak with her!* But Alexandra continues with the theme of the preceding scene (i.e., letting Big Dog be naughty). Charlotte then insists: *I want to speak to her.* And, with inspiration and tenderness in her voice, she follows up: *All day long I've been thinking of her. I want to see her.* But because Alexandra continues with Big Dog's pranks, Charlotte appeals to the public: *I want to talk to her. Who's going to take her?* But nobody responds. In desperation she then turns to her co-producer and, justifying her request, tells Alexandra firmly: *It's you that'll take her. You already have Fido, he's naughty. Just now he was naughty! Now you take him off!* Here is thus a succession of strategies; Charlotte tries to achieve what she wants by repetition and being very explicit, by seduction, by seeking support from the public, and finally by direct out-of-frame authority. In the end, Alexandra gives in and abandons Big Dog, but Charlotte still has to be very insistent and cries out: *Sophie! Sophie!* before Alexandra starts mobilizing Little Girl.

Thus, when the children want to have an idea accepted and run into a refusal or resistance from their partner, they find a variety of means to put their idea across. They produce a rich diversity of persuasive methods (delaying tactics, concessions, seduction, authority) even to the point of abandoning the theatrical frame and show their capacity to play on the feelings of their partner. The tact and skill should be noted with which these procedures are put into practice without offending the partner as if the main preoccupation was to avoid any kind of conflict that might put a stop to the show.

We would underline two essential aspects. First, the phase of reaching initial agreement is accomplished speedily and efficiently. It seems that the need to present the public with something interesting drives the children to be quick. They behave as if they knew very well that the startup cannot be prolonged indefinitely. How do they proceed? They do not announce the theme they are going to develop—there is no preparatory dialogue. Agreement is reached in the course of improvisation during the first few exchanges. Agreement may be achieved right from the first announcement whereupon the partner's rejoinder is already a step advancing the scenario. At other times, some dialogue is needed, either because the two partners do not understand one another or— and this is frequently the case—because one of the partners resists or refuses to adopt the other's proposal. To overcome an initial lack of comprehension, the children proceed to clarify, to explain, to be more explicit about their proposal. To persuade an unwilling partner, the children resort to negotiations with recourse to procedures that almost invariably are acted out theatrically. It seems that in the puppet shows they wish to avoid open conflict at any cost and in this they succeed.

Second, we would also underline that the negotiating strategies used by the children to overcome difficulties reveal their knowledge of the behavior and reactions of others. They are capable of understanding what their partner is thinking, wants, is sensitive to. It is possible that this understanding allows them better to control their own reactions to what their partner says and does, and that this remove from themselves brings them to begin to deal with problems of self and other.

INTERPERSONAL RELATIONSHIPS REFLECTED IN THE PUPPET SCENES

Once the theme is agreed on, the children go on to play scenes that are remarkable for their coherence. Although earlier studies brought out the cognitive processes that ensure this coherence (Stambak & Royon, 1985), this study is more concerned with content. An analysis of the scenes shows that their content relates to what the children understand of the social world around them. This concern is common to all symbolic play at our subjects' ages (cf. Bretherton, 1984). In puppet shows, however, the themes are not exactly the same as in other forms of symbolic play. Rather than focusing on the enactment of everyday events (meals, toilet, etc.) or on action sequences that typify certain persons (mother, cook, doctor, etc.), the children working the puppets are primarily concerned with the relationships between the characters portrayed. For sure, the background of many scenes is still the same round of routine activities similar to what is reported of nontheatrical play by numerous authors including Garvey (1982), Nelson and Seidman (1984), Stockinger-Forys and McCune-Nicolich (1984), but the dominant feature in the puppet scenes remains interindividual relations. The dramatic aspect of symbolic play underlined by Schwartzman (1978) and Forbes et al. (1986) is also very much present in children's puppet shows. No doubt it is the special nature of the puppet show, its theatrical side and the need to entertain the public that induces the children to present scenarios with well-defined characters whose relationships are portrayed at length. In order to retain the attention of the public it is not sufficient to present a flat account of a series of events or to reproduce some well-known activity. By creating on stage the relationships between various characters, the children succeed in rendering the scenes lively and attractive. By varying the relationships, they keep the story moving forward and at the same time reveal their psychosocial knowledge.

For our analysis of the interpersonal relationships as portrayed in the scenarios, we distinguished three kinds of plays: those dealing with authority as between educator and learner, those based on friendship or sympathy such as occurs between persons of equal status (whether children or adults) and, a class apart, those dealing with human beings and animals.

Authoritarian Relationships Between Educator and Learner

In the scenes presented in the following, two children give their puppets complementary roles with one puppet educating the other. Generally, the educating part concerns social regulations and the customs that govern the children's everyday life at home and in the kindergarten. In their improvised scenarios they deal with what is usual or, by contrast, with what is inadmissible in their daily experience. More than forbidden behavior, they portray the authoritarian relationship between two people of which one is trying to impose his point of view on the other; the relationship is displayed with great diversity.

Example 1.   Charlotte (3;4) and Alexandra (3;3) put on a show that is exemplary in this respect, for almost all the scenes are variations on the authority theme that the two girls enjoy acting out.

From the outset the two puppets establish an authoritarian relationship that may be called standard: The educator induces the learner to behave properly and to observe good manners. Charlotte's puppet is the authority trying to get Alexandra's puppet to wait her turn to eat and to eat correctly.

Charlotte, 3;4	Alexandra, 3;3
(works Clown called Momo = M)	(works Little Girl = LG)
	Looks at Charlotte: *Hey, he's gonna eat.* LG moves closer to the plate.
No, she says smiling. *The pancake isn't even made yet.* In a lower voice: *Momo'll be happy.* Turning to Alexandra: *Not yet*, and putting M on the plate: *He's not going to eat right now.*	
	Alexandra shakes her head in agreement.
She touches LG with her free hand: *Not yet, OK?*	
	She again shakes her head.
Takes M away from the plate.	
	Brings LG nearer to the plate.
Violently M. is put back on the plate preventing LG from coming closer.	
	LG is pulled back.
Lifts up M: *Now you can eat.*	
	LG dives onto the plate.

Cries: *Oooh!* as if LG had done something bad.	
	She mutters: *Dirty.*
Looks at M. with a knowing smile. Then, rather gently, she hits LG with M.	
	Also with a knowing look, Alexandra drops LG out of sight and says in reproachful tones: *Go to bed!* She abandons the puppet.
Abandons the puppet.	

Various strategies are used illustrating the way an educator generally proceeds: The rules are stated, one makes sure they are understood, there is supervision to see they are followed, and punishment when they are not. In this example, the learner is obedient, even submissive, bends to the rules, and accepts punishment without protest.

In the next scene, the relationship is different—the educator no longer manages to be obeyed, for this time the learner is not an obedient child but a recalcitrant character even to the point of provocation. To represent him, Alexandra chooses Big Dog who misbehaves (*Oh, he's eaten all the flowers!*) and, despite being rebuked, commits the offense two times more.

Then, in Scene 3, Charlotte tries to persuade Alexandra to give up the rebellious Big Dog in favor of Little Girl, hoping perhaps that in this way the teacher will find it easier to be obeyed (cf. pp. 105–106). Because Charlotte is very insistent, Alexandra gives in, but, unlike in Scene 1, Little Girl is no longer docile but also resists . . .

Charlotte	Alexandra
(holds Little Boy)	(holds Little Girl)
	She dashes LG onto the plate and takes her off again immediately, looking at Charlotte.
Oh, you're naughty all the same. Go to bed! She hits LG with LB. *You do a lot of naughty things!* and hits her again.	
	She looks at LG and touches the puppet's dress.
In severe tones: *Go to bed!*	
	Oh, no!

So no more nonsense from you, OK? Severe
voice.

> Loud voice: *Yes!* and she promptly
> puts LG back onto the plate.

Now you're going to go to bed.

> Drops LG out of view: *OK*.

[They change puppets.]

Faced with resistance, Charlotte shows that she well understands the various ways of dealing with a disobedient child. The character she portrays alternates between severity with punishment and moralizing tones (*You do a lot of
naughty things!*) and also tries to elicit a promise (*So no more nonsense from you,
OK?*). But Alexandra also knows a bit about disobedience; as the learner, she
insists on breaking the established rule and does not readily accept punishment, so much so that the balance of power is in danger of being inverted.

In the subsequent scene, Alexandra heightens the pitch of disobedience by
again using Big Dog, the symbol of rebellion. He refuses to obey orders and
in the end attacks his master and bites him. The master plays being bitten
with many an *Ouch! ouch!* and is obviously badly hurt. Authority is overcome
by revolt.

It was a surprise to see the two puppeteers change roles in their last scene.
The inversion is discussed later with reference to knowledge of interpersonal
relations and theatrical conventions.

The impressive variety of educator–learner relationships enacted by the two
puppeteers was rendered possible by Alexandra accepting to play the learner,
which is fairly rare. It perhaps explains why in the end they exchange roles
adopting a more or less symmetrically shared distribution.

Example 2.   The next example illustrates knowledge of another aspect of
authoritarian relations between child and adult. The puppeteers play out a scene
in which a spoiled girl asks her father for candy and succeeds by wheedling
in getting the upper hand.

Elisa, 3;3   Noëline, 3;2

Takes on Bear.   Has Little Girl.

What happened to . . . children?
Turns B towards LG.
What happened?

What happened? She touches LG with her hand. Her expression is one of enquiry.

Shows LG and brings her near B. She chirrups: *Oh Daddy, say, would you please buy some candy?*

Oh! She makes B disappear, then brings him out again, with munching noises. Approaches LG with B and touches LG as if giving her something.

Implores: *Candy, daddy, candy!*

Oh, plaintively, while retreating LG. *You hurt my teeth.* She hits B with LG. Turns LG toward herself, looks at her sadly, lays her down on the edge of the ''stage,'' then lies down on top of her with a long-suffering expression.

Oh! regretfully. Takes off B and with her bare hand picks up a pot from behind the theatre and holds it out to LG.

Noëline does not react.

Tries to lift up LG's head.

Shakes LG apparently as a kind of refusal. Then takes off LG and takes up Little Dog. Says: *That's the dog*, and for a long while lets him eat out of the pot.

Bends down to pick up another puppet.

This scene puts the accent on psychological features of the characters portrayed. Having an indulgent father, the daughter gives free rein to her whims. Once she has obtained the candy, she complains of having been aggressed, she hits out and then goes into a sulk. She circumvents authority by cunning and the person in authority complacently falls in with her tricks.

Some of the scenes played by Marie (3;0) and Julie (3;0) also put on stage the educator–learner relationship. What is shown this time is talk and action between two educators on the subject of how to be obeyed and what punishment would fit the learner's transgression. Two examples are given here of how the two educators working together react to misbehavior committed by Big Dog.

In the first, two educators—represented by Little Boy and Man—have to deal with a problem of cleanliness.

Marie, 3;0

She has Little Boy on her hand and Big Dog under her arm.

Animating LB she says: *Wait, will you wait. I have to change him, he's done poo-poo.* She talks of BD as if he were a child.

Indicates her approval mischievously and with complicity.

Looks at Julie and in turn disapproves: *Oh, no!*

Looks at Julie with mischievous expression.

Puts BD onto her hand.

Just wait . . . you'll be scolded. She puts BD on the edge of the "stage" and with LB lifts up and pulls down BD's garment while holding BD's head. *Poo-bang!* and she hits him on the snout. *There, he's been scolded.* Then she lifts the two puppets to her face. *There now, he's quite clean!*

Yes. She brings forward her two puppets letting them dance and sing: *Too-too, when you do poo-poo, when you do poo-poo.* She looks at the camera as if in expectation.

Julie, 3;0

She holds Man.

Interested, she turns toward the audience and moves M. *Fido's done poo-poo, what?*

Yes he's done poo-poo, in a very low voice, and then: *You've done poo-poo, Fido, oh no!* And she beats BD with M.

No! with a severe expression. To the audience: *You can . . . Fido did poo-poo in his pants.*

Look . . . to the audience.

Turns M toward BD: *In his pants.* She looks fixedly at Marie.

Is he quite clean? in a very small voice. She turns M toward the other two puppets.

In this scene, the two educators are in agreement that the misbehavior calls for punishment. But they seem to realize that the transgression is not very serious. It is more like an accident, there was no deliberate naughtiness and after the punishment there is immediate consolation. The two children's capacity for generalization should also be noted. The last line (that's what happens every time you misbehave like that) is a kind of conclusion that sums up all that was said before and in a way makes the scene an exemplar of all the scenes of this kind.

A little later in the same show, the two educators face a different problem, namely a child who does not want to go to sleep. Here, the educators' behavior is different. The puppet representing the child is no longer totally passive but has become a character who puts up resistance that those in authority have to take into account. The educator–learner relationship calls for a little persuasion and, once the desired result is obtained, leads to reward.

After having changed the child (still represented by Big Dog) who had peed in the bed, one of the "adults" covers him up: *There, he's asleep.* Whereupon the other proposes: *OK, let's go fix some food.* Her partner having agreed to the proposal, she says: *We won't wake him up.* But the child does wake up.

Marie	Julie
She holds Little Girl and puts Big Dog down on the edge of the "stage." She makes LG disappear and then brings her up again saying: *Oh, is waking up,* with reference to BD.	Holds Little Boy
	Brings LB close to BD. Displeased: *Oh, no!*
Scolds: *Oh no!*	

[Together, LG and LB beat BD.]

	LB turns to the audience: *We spanked him, we did! He's not nice!*
Oh, no! She puts him back down and smacks him.	
	He woke up!
So he woke up, did he? Turning to the public: *Fido you're going back to bed.*	
	LB takes hold of BD's head. Authoritatively: *You are going to bed, OK?*

Julie then goes on to explain: *Even we'd like to go to sleep.* To achieve her end, Mary changes tactics and with tenderness pretends to dress BD in his pajamas and to tuck him in. *Now he's asleep. You'll see, he won't wake up now.* The two puppeteers then pretend to go to sleep themselves and start snoring. When later on the child wakes up at the right time, he is entitled to a reward. *We'll give you a big present!* says the one. *A big present, big big!* says the other.

Just as Charlotte and Alexandra did in their show, Marie and Julie avoid giving a one-sided view of authority. To deal with misbehavior that is not too serious they use complex educational methods with a mixture of firmness and tenderness. Between the two puppeteers playing similar roles there is an element of sympathy that is commented on later.

The various scenes dealing with authority allow the observer to evaluate young children's knowledge of how adults try to get children to obey the rules of everyday life as well as how children go about coping with the demands made by the adults.

It is quite clear that the children understand the gamut of requirements that the adults try to teach them. One eats and goes to sleep at certain times, there are certain rituals that have to be observed, one has to be clean. Infringements are more or less reprehensible depending on whether they were more or less intentional, and punishments may accordingly be more or less severe.

More than in the various interdictions they are faced with, the children seem to be interested in the relationships between adults and children. By putting different characters on stage the children portray a whole scale of educator-learner relationships with varying balance of power. They mobilize severe authoritarians dealing with learners who are in turn submissive, teasing, disobedient, or even rebellious. But tolerant, even feeble educators are also portrayed and the children know very well how to exploit them. The variety of tactics used by the educators is also noteworthy. They make rules, rebuke, and punish the disobedient, but can also be moralizing and even offer gifts by way of reward. The scenes show that the children know perfectly well that there are different tactics for dealing with orders, and that authority can be resisted or even circumvented.

The relationships are made dramatic and emphasis is used in many different ways to intensify conflictual situations. The theatrical context of course lends itself to such treatment and ringing the changes on interpersonal relations is evidently an effective way of interesting the audience.

Portraying Sympathy and Friendship

In other shows, the children expressed affinity, friendly relations, and mutual understanding between people of similar status. To analyze the scenes with these characteristics, we took greater account of facial expressions, intonations, movements, and postures of the puppeteers than in analyzing other kinds of scenes (it will be recalled that the top half of the puppeteers is visible from the audience). Sympathy and friendship were staged in different ways, of which we distinguished three: affective participation when characters exert themselves to say and do the same things; complicity when they express identical points of view and identical judgments regarding a third person; and teasing when the game is to make sure that, whatever the successive provocations, preexisting understanding is not diminished. Further analysis of these different kinds of friendly relationships is given later. The tone of the shows is merry, which strongly suggests that the children take pleasure in acting friendship and understanding.

Affective Participation. Friendly relationships are shown in the kind of show we call *musicals* (cf. Bréauté et al. 1987): The children get the puppets to sing and dance together, which generally serves as an intermezzo between scenes. A kind of affective communion is clearly shared by the two children. Their movements and especially their facial expression bear witness to their pleasure in having the puppets act similarly and in the same rhythm. One might even say that the musicals express a state of emotional contagion.

Even more striking in the register of sympathy are the occasional scenarios in which emotional sharing is the very theme. The children portray characters who show their agreement by giving expression to their similarity.

Marie (3;0) and Julie (3;0) create a scene around a birthday. The two characters they portray show that they are of the same age. Then one of them plays in unison with the other by imitating both her actions and speech. They share the ritual of the birthday celebration that is concluded with song and dance as well as congratulations and general merriment.

Marie has two puppets, Big Dog and Little Girl. She starts the scene by waving Big Dog at the audience: . . . *that's Fido, he's 3½ years old.* Julie, who is holding Little Boy, immediately continues by waving her puppet in turn and saying energetically: *I'm 3 years old I am.* Little Girl follows suit by announcing: *I'm 3 years old.* Little Boy, as if prompted by what Little Girl says, introduces the birthday party idea: *I'm 3 years to have my birthd . . .* He goes down behind the theater and comes up with a puppet that he shows to the audience and that represents the birthday cake. Cheerfully he announces: *Look at my birthday, yah!* Little Girl disappears in turn looking for another cake. *Look at my birthday!* she hurries to say. Little Boy dives down several times as if he were preparing the birthday feast: *There the plate . . . there yummy . . . and there and there!* he comments feverishly. *And there,* Little Girl echoes carrying out the same gestures. Three times more Little Boy dives down and seems to place something on the cake (no doubt birthday candles). He announces gaily: *One, two . . .* and Little Girl completes the count: *Three!* The two characters then rush to the cake and blow out the candles.

Having explained their age and their perfect agreement about the birthday ritual, the party proper can begin. The two puppets sing and dance, they embrace and congratulate one another, and portray the happy conviviality of an enjoyable party. Then they turn to the audience and one of the puppets comments the "emotional contagion": *We danced well, didn't we?*

In this particularly lively scene, there is the great satisfaction one can experience in sharing an activity and in feeling oneself to be similar to and in total harmony with another person. Little Girl shows her interest in and approval of Little Boy's ideas by her echoing responses, which encourage Little Boy to continue the scene with increasing enthusiasm. Between the two, an affective and emotional resonance establishes itself which is all the more telling because of the pleasure and joy expressed by the body movements and facial expressions of the two puppeteers.

In scenes of this type and in the musicals, the children exert their ability to share emotions. They clearly understand the sympathy that arises when one is in emotional harmony with another person.

Close Partnership. In other scenes, the children represent agreement between characters and the sympathy arising from identity of views and ideas. Generally, two educators are portrayed who agree on how to deal with naughty children.

One example was already related, that is, the scene where Marie (3;0) and Julie (3;0) have their two puppets, Little Girl and Little Boy, represent two educators who are in perfect agreement about the seriousness of the transgression and the consequent punishment of a child who has "done poo-poo in his pants." The agreement is evident from the puppeteers' mischievous facial expressions and the looks of complicity they exchange. The close partnership between these two "educators" is further underlined by their calling on the audience to agree with their assessment of the transgression.

The second example is taken from a different show. Following a long negotiation, Maria (3;6) and Stéphane (2;8) also create the pretense of two educators who have to deal with the same situation and who react in unison. This time, however, the puppeteers themselves played the educators, the children being represented by puppets, but the puppets were not put on the hand in the usual way.

Maria hits Little Boy and announces: *He's done poo-poo*. Stéphane goes further with Little Girl: *He's done poo-poo, we'll scold him, we'll bend him*. This last suggestion is perhaps the origin of the odd turn the scene now takes. Each child goes about folding the puppets. *There you are*, Maria takes up the idea, *we'll bend him*. She even rolls her puppet into a ball. *Come on*, she says, *we'll do it like that*. She is immediately followed by Stéphane who repeats: *We'll do it like that*. Laughing more and more, the children end up with an unexpected punishment: *Come on*, Maria proposes, *we'll put him in the garbage*, whereupon she throws Little Boy down behind her. Following Maria's lead, Stéphane bursts out: *We'll put him in the garbage!* And in turn he throws Little Girl over his shoulder.

The characteristic of these scenes is that the children play identical characters thereby expressing their agreement, the actions and utterances of the characters being the same. As Maria and Stéphane's scenario progresses toward derision, the ridiculous representation of the educators brings out the close partnership between the puppeteers. The educators become funny people and are perhaps also meant as a parody of authority in general. In this scene too, the laughter of the puppeteers, their exaggerated facial expressions, the grand way they make their pronouncements with the backing of the audience, all bear witness to the complicity of the puppeteers in dealing with a third person and no doubt also to their mockery of accepted values.

Teasing. Under the heading of sympathy and friendship we included scenes in which the children play companions who enjoy going against one another but who do it without malice and who know "it's just for fun." All the provocations cannot hide the deep understanding and mutual knowledge that binds friends together.

This form of relationship is illustrated by examples taken from three shows created by three pairs of children between the ages of 3 and 4. As is seen, the mastery of this complex form of give-and-take progresses with age.

Julie (3;0) manipulates Little Boy; Marie (3;0) manipulates Little Girl and Big Dog. In an aside, Julie suggests that the puppet that Little Boy has placed in front of him on the edge of the theater should be stolen: *Go take it.* She then manipulates Little Boy and lets him dance without a care, just so that the theft will be easy to carry out. After a moment's hesitation, Little Girl and Big Dog take the puppet. Little Boy thereupon becomes agitated in a disorderly way and goes hither and thither as if he were looking everywhere for his stolen possession. Not finding it, he starts to whimper. Little Girl immediately gives back the puppet, which falls to the ground, and the two puppeteers start laughing.

This little scene, which is the final one in a show, illustrates the teasing relationship in which the theft of the puppet is done "as a joke" because the two girls express their enjoyment at the end.

The next example is taken from a show put on by Diane (3;4) and Noëline (3;2). Noëline manipulates Clown; Diane manipulates Grandmother. The two puppets go about making a birthday cake. Clown collects the necessary equipment and is assisted by Grandmother who passes him the utensils. At one point, Clown, addressing the audience in a squeaky voice, gives his partner an occasion to go in for teasing. *Who*, he says, *has taken my spoons?* Grandmother seems to give them back to him, but then makes them disappear inside the theater. Clown is at first bewildered, but then asks again: *Who has taken the red one?* This time Grandmother produces the requested object: *There it is*, she says. Clown seems surprised by this rapid result. Then, in order to keep the situation alive,

the audience takes a hand: *It's the little dog who has taken the spoons. It's Bonzo!*
From this point on, the two puppeteers clearly go in for the teasing relationship. Diane abandons Grandmother and takes up Little Dog whom she waves
at the audience with a big smile, while Clown pretends to be looking everywhere for the culprit: *Bonzo, Bonzo, where's Bonzo?* Little Dog hides behind the
theater. Clown still pretends to be looking for him and finally concludes: *He's
not there.* At that moment Little Dog does appear and shows himself to Clown.
To finish the scene, the two girls together tap their puppets on the edge of the
theater.

In this scene, as long as she was manipulating Grandmother, Diane hesi-
tated to let her puppet be an all-out teaser. Do grandmothers really steal spoons?
But when the audience suggests that Little Dog is the thief, she gives up working Grandmother and, with Little Dog, fully adopts the role of the practical
joker, which is well accentuated by her mischievous facial expression, body
movements, and tone of voice. In this way, the children clearly show that the
theft was just for fun.

In another show, Alexandre (3;8) and Clément (4;0) play a lengthy show
in which the characters tease one another consistently. They respectively
manipulate Little Dog and Bear, who represent two friends going off camp-
ing. Little Dog plays the busy organizer getting everything ready for departure, while Bear concentrates on teasing. Right from the start, the two characters
are well established. While the eager organizer is busy filling a basket with
things needed for the trip, the teaser declares in tones making it clear that even
he regards the idea as off-beat: *I'm . . . well I'm going to . . . I'm going to have
a lie-down.* This incongruity makes the children laugh. Then the organizer takes
up his proper role again and puts the other one back in his place: *Hold it, hey,
hold it. We haven't got there yet. We still have to take the train and . . . our stuff, all
our stuff.*

Here again we are in the humorous vein. By their laughter, the children
show that the characters recognize as a joke the suggestion of going to lie down.

Following this initial skirmish, the two characters give expression to their
friendship and to the pleasure they take in their joint project by means of repetition and identical emphases as described in previous sections. *We'll have a
lot to carry*, says the teaser. *You bet*, confirms the organizer. *Both of us*, the teaser
gently adds. *You bet*, his partner repeats.

From this point on, each gives as good as he gets.

With an impish look, the teaser steals the basket his partner has been filling
conscientiously. This time the organizer finds a way to take the wind out of
his partner by pretending to interpret it as assistance. He teases his companion by reacting as if the basket had been taken for the purpose of carrying it.
Pointing to an object that has not yet been loaded, the organizer says: *Teddy
Bear, wait for that!* The teaser brings back the basket and only then, when his
goods have been returned to him, does the organizer reprimand his compan-

ion: *Naughty!* The latter deprecates this announcement: *No,* he says, *not naughty,* and proceeds to laugh.

After these frolics, it is the organizer's turn to play a trick on his partner. Having emptied the basket of its contents, the organizer incites his friend to repeat the theft and tries to provoke him as follows: *The basket, you won't touch it, OK? It's delicate!* The teaser sure enough falls for it and steals the empty basket. The organizer then makes his point: *There's nothing in it.* But the teaser finds a way to trump his partner's trick. He dips his hand into the basket, pretends to find some object and comes up with "it" saying: *It's my little toy!* [In French: *C'est ma surprise!* i.e., a free gift that comes with cereal, for example.]

Following these pleasantries, there is an interlude during which the characters congratulate one another and take up their common project again.

Going in for reciprocal provocations and responding to them with rejoinders that thicken the plot, the two characters develop their teasing relationship with considerable mastery. They display mutual knowledge and show great tolerance for each other as well as a kind of complicity that bears witness to their profound agreement, which they nevertheless explicitly reaffirm in the course of the interludes.

The scenes that incorporate the teasing element seemed to us, despite the oppositional tendency, to be pursued in an atmosphere of sympathy and friendship. The analysis shows that among the youngest subjects the aspect "for the fun of it" is already well mastered. Among older children, the theme is developed at greater length and with greater diversification. They show themselves capable of provoking the provoker and of foiling a provocation. The facilitating role of certain puppets (Bear, Little Dog, Big Dog) may also be noted. These are the puppets that usually are allowed to misbehave in the shows the children have seen put on by the adults and are thus more easily cast by the children in the role of jokers.

In these scenes, provocation and appeasement alternate as if the children were conscious of the need to maintain agreement through knowledge of others and knowledge of self. They show mastery of the emotional reaction of others and of how to bring it about. By giving themselves the means to avoid rupture, they indicate how highly they value agreement. It is as if they knew that constantly putting it to the test gives friendship its full meaning.

The children show clearly in these friendship scenes that they are aware of the pleasure that can be experienced by being in harmony with someone else. To try an experiment together, to share emotions, to understand one another, to reach agreement, these would seem to be the essential contents of such scenes. The children have apparently understood that this participation, whether affective or intellectual, can be put to use in the creation of amusing scenes. The means employed to this end are altogether appropriate, especially the joyous emphasis in intonation and facial expression.

In peer interaction, the children can express their knowledge of the other.

Alike and at the same time different, the other is the one with whom one shares emotions and ideas, but whom one may also oppose and with whom one progresses in knowledge and sentiment.

Relations Between Humans and Animals

It will be noted that the available animal puppets are not always used as animals by the children. In several of the scenes described, the animals represent humans. Big Dog plays the part of a young child in the scene invented by Marie and Julie. Similarly, Noëline assigns to Bear the role of a father giving his daughter candy.

In what follows, we look at instances where children use animal puppets more as animals and base their scenes on relations with animals, especially cat and dog. It will be seen that the relations between animals and humans are strongly colored emotionally.

The first example shows affective participation in which a cat plays a role. It is part of the show put on by Marie (3;0) and Julie (3;0), and constitutes a kind of intermezzo following a violent episode in which Big Dog devoured Clown. Julie announces the entry of her puppet: *There's little cat,* and marks her presence with a plaintive meow. Marie, who is manipulating Man, reacts to the plaintive tone of the cat by having Man adopt a sympathetic attitude. He questions the cat on her unhappiness: *Tell me, dear, why are you crying?* Little Cat replies in catlike tones: *I'm tired.* Man then explains his fellow feeling: *Oh, me too, I also the same, I'm the same.* After these shared endearments, the two characters comfort one another by embracing.

In this scene, the cat appears as an animal that arouses tender feelings. Being feeble and vulnerable, it induces the human being to be protective and to show fondness.

Relations with a dog can be more complex as in the following example. It will be recalled that in the show put on by Charlotte (3;4) and Alexandra (3;3), the girls portray the authority relationship with Little Girl as learner at one time, and Big Dog at another. The learner, as long as the part is played by Little Girl, remains docile and submissive. By contrast, Big Dog goes against the authority of the teacher and even becomes a rebel to the point of going over to physical attack.

Thomas (3;6) and Yohanna (3;4) put on a show entirely devoted to relationships with a dog who, as will be seen, can be a friendly companion but also a dangerous animal.

In the first scene, Thomas immediately stages a dog that threatens, a frightening dog. Fear, it should be noted, is portrayed only in scenes that include Big Dog. At no time did any child or adult character try to frighten any other human. It should also be noted that, in the shows put on for the children by the kindergarten staff, Big Dog has a special status as the one who misbehaves and is rebuked in consequence, but who is never aggressive. It follows that when the children bring fear of a dog into their show, they are reflecting their own preoccupations.

Having to face this dog, who seems on the point of attacking, Yohanna acts out a series of possible countermoves. She first works Little Girl, but her puppet is bitten by Big Dog and runs away. Then she presents Little Boy who is more courageous and faces up to the animal. He calls out to the dog, hits him, but in the end is also bitten. Yohanna then confronts Big Dog with Bear. Bear hits, but Big Dog bites back, perhaps recognizing an adversary worth taking on. Between the two, there follows a fairly well-matched fight that ends in a merry brawl with the animals snapping at one another.

Using different puppets, Yohanna thus right from the start sketches the main attitudes one can adopt toward a dangerous animal: being afraid and running away, or putting up resistance. Standing up to the animal, it will be noted, is easier if the animal's opponent is another animal rather than a human being.

The numerous scenes that follow introduce subtle variations on relations with a dog. The dog also changes his ways in response to certain behaviors of his human partner.

In the second scene, Yohanna again takes up Little Girl, who now plays the part of a stern master. Bitten by Big Dog, who continues to be manipulated by Thomas, Little Girl hits the dog and rebukes him: *Bad dog!* She keeps him at a distance and voices his name, Bonzo, in different tones in order to calm him, to threaten him and also to rebuke him. To put an end to the rebukes, Big Dog then changes his behavior. He tries to cajole his master into caring for him and looking after him.

Thomas	Yohanna
He holds Big Dog	She holds Little Girl and Bear.
Dashes Big Dog toward Little Girl. Looks at BD's tongue, then turning to the audience pulls BD's tongue, and points to his open snout saying: *He's thirsty*.	
	Beats BD with LG.
BD repeats his request by pretending to drink.	
	Bear comes forward and says: *OK, I brought you a glass of water*, and puts his paw on the edge of the theater.

He slides BD to the spot where B has
put the water and drinks.

She brings on LG who taps on the
theater and orders: *You're going to lie
down.*

BD runs away from LG but then lies
down motionless in front of B and LG.

B and LG rush to BD saying: *Bonzo,
lie down!* She then hits BD on the head
with B: *Shut your eyes, shut your mouth,*
while LG supervises the situation.

He lifts up BD, hides him behind the
theater and looks at the audience with
a satisfied expression.

Working two puppets during this scene, Yohanna succeeds in differentiat-
ing the role of master: Little Girl plays the severe, impersonal master who gives
the orders, whereas Bear shows greater kindness and attends to Big Dog's needs.

In the next scene, the children present an encounter between animals. Bear
is walking peacefully (does he thus incite pursuit?) and hides at the approach
of Big Dog. In this scene, the children clearly show their familiarity with certain characteristics of a dog. For example, when the dog stays still, Thomas
comments: *He is smelling . . . he smells the . . . the bear.* Thomas evidently knows
how a hunting dog follows his prey.

In the scene after that, Thomas' Big Dog continues in menacing vein oppo-
site Little Boy held by Yohanna. This time the relationship between human
being and animal reaches a balance. The children have their puppets impersonate characters who frighten one another. Big Dog attacks Little Boy and
bites him. Little Boy scolds the dog and hits him. Each threatens the other
and both then hide for protection. The action is repeated several times and
ends in a relationship being established in which neither has the upper hand.
By advancing and retreating, each character expresses a reciprocity that the
children comment upon at the end of the scene: Thomas waves Big Dog at
the audience saying: *He's afraid . . . he's afraid of Nicholas,* while Yohanna hides
Little Boy behind her back saying: *Nicholas, he's afraid of Bonzo.*

In this example the children show they understand that relationships with
a dog depend on how the dog behaves: One does not behave in the same way
with a friendly dog as with an aggressive dog. The puppeteers seem particularly concerned when the dog becomes threatening. Fear then dominates the
scene. They know that a range of strategies can be followed. With a nonthreaten-
ing dog, dependence on the master is brought to the fore, a master of whom
the dog may also be afraid.

Staging the relationship between humans and animals allows the children to express strongly colored emotions. Their main preoccupation seems to be their fear of the dog. While treating fear in its various facets, the theatrical fiction allows them to master it.

OBJECTIVIZING PSYCHOSOCIAL KNOWLEDGE THROUGH THE THEATER

Our various analyses bring out how capable the children are in inventing scenarios and getting their puppets to play the appropriate characters. Their dramatic ability seems to us to go together with full realization that the fictive creation enjoys an independent existence from which the actors are able to detach themselves. Certain significant theatrical procedures attest to the distance the young authors can maintain from their productions. They may, for example, replay a scene with reversal of roles, or condense the contents of a scene retaining only outstanding facts or salient events.

We believe that the distance separating them from their productions enables the children to objectivize the psychosocial knowledge displayed in their scenarios.

Charlotte and Alexandra's show (see the detailed account of some episodes pp. 90–92) in which the two children develop a range of relationships vis-à-vis authority is exemplary in this respect. Toward the end of their show they take up again the contents of the two previous scenes, combining them and exchanging the roles symmetrically.

Scene 1. The first of these scenes is concerned with the relationship of submission to authority. Alexandra manipulates Little Girl and tries to get her to eat. Charlotte, who manipulates Clown, prevents it, and with many a directive and threatening gesture repeats her interdiction. Alexandra, in the end, abandons her efforts to feed Little Girl and meekly waits for permission. The scene ends with the punishment of Little Girl who is sent to bed on account of her messy eating.

Scene 2. One of the following scenes is concerned with negotiation when there is revolt against authority. The matter at issue is again eating and Charlotte is still in authority. Alexandra, who holds Little Girl, dashes her provokingly onto the plate, and Charlotte, who holds Little Boy, rebukes her: *Oh, you're naughty!* and orders her to go to bed. Alexandra tries at first to avert her partner's attention but then refuses boldly to follow orders. So Charlotte attempts a compromise: *No more nonsense from you, OK?*, but this also is rejected by Alexandra. At the end of the scene, the punishment is accepted.

Scene 3. In the last scene, the main lines of Scenes 1 and 2 are picked up again with inversion of the roles played by the puppeteers and condensation of the scenario. The children work the same puppets as in Scene 2, but now it is Charlotte who misbehaves and puts herself in the role previously acted by Alexandra. Taking up Scene 1 again, she announces while manipulating Little Boy: *He's going to eat.* She shoves a plate toward Alexandra encouraging her to respond to the provocation. Alexandra thereupon takes up the role of authority previously held by Charlotte. *Don't eat the pancake*, Alexandra orders. *Stop!* she continues. She rebukes: *Naughty!* and punishes: *You go to bed*, while Charlotte in turn represents submission to orders and punishment, although, by way of counterpoint recalling Scene 2, she has her moment of resistance.

Scene 3 thus recapitulates the two preceding ones. There are differences between Scenes 1 and 2 and their reproduction in Scene 3. All the features were not taken up again; lines were not repeated in their entirety; the sequence of events was not always respected. Because of these differences it could be maintained that by introducing variations and exchanging roles the children created a new scene. But—and this is of the essence—they retained the salient points of the action and reproduced the key elements of the dialogue that sustain the coherence of the story. The contents are the same, as are the situations. Above all, the sense of the interpersonal relationship—the thrust and parry within the authority–submission frame—is the same. The children also retained the lines and gestures that best delineate their respective roles. Although they do some pruning, they stay close to the original, even to the point of prompting the partner about the next move or spoken line in order to keep the action going. Charlotte, for example, prompts Alexandra on a line she, Charlotte, used in one of the preceding scenes: *You say . . . you say . . . that I'll do no more nonsense*, which now fits the role of Alexandra who immediately complies. Each actor strives to reproduce the gestures and lines produced by the other in previous scenes so that the coherence of the roles and the relationship between the two characters is preserved despite the inversion of cast.

In the example just analyzed, there appear a number of typically theatrical procedures—repetition of scenes with inversion of roles, reformulation of repeated elements, condensation, highlighting of main dramatic features—which yield a new scene. But, as already pointed out, the new is closely modeled on the original and, although variations are introduced, they remain faithful to what went before.

What do these productions tell us about the young puppeteers' understanding of theatrical convention?

1. On the theatrical production level properly speaking:

   - The children show themselves capable of abstracting the most important points of the story line. They grasp the pivotal points and whatever elements are essential for coherence.

   - They can reproduce an action while condensing and accelerating it, and reducing it to its essentials.

2. The children show that they are conscious of the fictional nature of their productions and of the underlying rules.

- They are cognizant of the arbitrary aspect of their productions: A certain role is not definitively attributed to a certain actor. Once they have agreed to vary the show, either of the puppeteers may take any role. The ease with which such changes are accomplished is noteworthy. Between the children there is an immediate adjustment, without announcement, without previous arrangement.

- The children do not identify themselves with the roles they create and interpret, but remain aware of the fact that they are acting. When, for example, they exchange roles of authority and submission, each takes up the characteristics and way of talking of the newly adopted role with smooth ability.

- They are cognizant of the permanent aspect of their productions. A text, a scene exists with its own coherence and dramatic energy independent of when it was produced, and it can thus be repeated. Charlotte accordingly prompts Alexandra on the line that needs to be spoken at a given moment of the dialogue.

It may be said that the interchangeability of roles and the capacity to condense the story bear witness to a complex mental representation of the relationship between the author–actor and the fiction produced. It seems that in thus manifesting their ability to distance themselves from the theatrical fiction, our young puppeteers detach themselves also from the content matter of their productions. Via the repetition, inversion, and condensation of scenes, they deepen and objectivize their knowledge of interpersonal relations.

In the example analyzed, the children show by inverting the roles that they see authority as giving rise to complex relationships between individuals whose position may be varied, each character in turn becoming dominant or submissive. The awareness to which such inversion of roles may lead could very well assist the children in dealing with similar relationships in real life. It should also be underlined that not only do the children show varied and detailed knowledge of the authority relationship, but they are also capable of reproducing at will the interpersonal strategies acted out in previous scenes. They also behave as if they were quite familiar with the strategies one can deploy when faced with the imposition of a social rule. Taking one's distance from these interactive procedures undoubtedly contributes to enhanced mastery of social interaction.

CONCLUDING REMARKS

The analyses presented concern performances by pairs of 3-year-old children improvising puppet shows. These shows are a form of shared pretend play but of a particular kind because the children do not just play for themselves but for an audience; so one can speak of theatrical pretend play. Pretense is inherent in such a task: as soon as the children accept to be puppeteers, they enter the world of make-believe.

In the theatrical situation, as for that matter in any form of collective pretend play, one can distinguish (a) times when the children try to agree to an idea or play theme—this may give rise to real negotiations in view of reaching agreement; and (b) times when the idea agreed upon is developed more or less at length. In the theatrical situation, the children develop dramatic story lines with a coherence that is all the more striking because they improvise the scenario.

In this study we have tried to give definition to the social and psychosocial knowledge that these young children evince during both the agreement phase and the development phase.

Psychosocial Knowledge in the Agreement Phase

What is most striking is the speed with which the children installed behind the puppet theater manage to agree on the theme they are going to develop together. This applies at the outset, but also at the beginning of each scene.

At the age of 3 or so, the children do not announce the content of the scene they are going to play but define the theme by some spoken exchanges following an initial proposal.

Sometimes agreement is immediate. Working one or several puppets, one of the children proposes an idea. The partner gears in with a reply that in some way develops the first idea, and so, from the word go, the show gets under way. The children do this with such ease that one may not realize how great an achievement it represents. Their accomplishment in fact implies complex communicative and cognitive competences. To be able to respond so effectively, the partner must have perfectly understood the fictional content intended by the initiator. The communicative means used (utterances, gestures, postures, facial expressions) have to be correctly decoded. An occasional failure in fact highlights the difficulties the children have to overcome. It does happen, although rarely, that the partner fails to understand the initial proposal and asks for further details. Then it may be observed with what eagerness the initiator responds in order to clarify or explain the intention. This explanatory phase is brief and effective, and clearly brings out the children's remarkable capacity for mutual adjustment in deciding on a theme.

In our view, such a course of events would not be possible unless it be admitted that the children during the time they have spent in the kindergarten have already worked out a common frame of reference that facilitates mutual adjustments. It is by virtue of such a common frame that they succeed so quickly in attributing meaning to their partner's utterances and in signifying their eventual agreement.

In other scenes, the first reaction of the partner is to refuse the idea proposed by the initiator. In expressing disagreement, the responder acts as if his or her interests and desires of the moment differed from those of the initiator. The children are then observed to go in for a genuine process of negotiation: They exchange several propositions before coming to an agreement.

How do they manage to have their intention accepted? It may be said that their main strategy is interpersonal persuasion. Every means is used to achieve their end—playing for time, concession, seduction, authority. But it must be emphasized that the children behave as if at all costs they were intent on avoiding sharp conflict. Negotiations proceed gently. In the end, one of the children gives in and agreement is reached. There is thus an absence of violent oppositional or untimely self-assertive moves, frequent although such moves may be at this age (Bonica, chapter 3, this volume; Wallon, 1949). Do the children possibly realize that sharp conflict may block the show? Whatever the answer, it will be observed that it is within the fictional frame and thanks to theatrical means that the young partners succeed in going beyond their initial disagreement. The children act as if they recognized the need to agree on a theme in order to put on a show.

The search for agreement is especially remarkable in the show put on by two children of relatively large difference in age (2;10 vs. 3;6). In the course of a lengthy negotiation, the older child gradually realizes that sharing a theme with someone younger is not the same as doing so with a child one's own age. She has to proceed tentatively and seek adequate strategies, for she is faced with misunderstandings and refusals. She fails in her efforts to help or guide her younger partner, who does not take her suggestions into account. Not until she accepts a proposal made by the younger child are the two of them able to develop a scene together.

The creation of a puppet show by two children is thus particularly conducive to learning about negotiation. In this phase, the children practice regulating their utterances by adjusting to what the other says.

These reciprocal adjustment processes leading to agreement contribute in our view to consolidate interaction capacity as well as knowledge of relations between self and other. The speed with which the children react to their partner's interventions implies that they are competent interpreters of the other's utterances, facial expressions, body language, and even intonation. During negotiations, their interpretation covers not only the eventual fictional content but also the partner's degree of resistance to what has been proposed. The children thus learn to recognize what their partner is receptive to and what may be resisted; in order to have their own ideas accepted, they learn to take the other's wishes and intentions into account.

The diversity of strategies the children use to make themselves understood and to convince their partner is worth recalling: they clarify, specify, and justify their proposals; they use seduction and authoritativeness, and make concessions for the purpose of having their idea accepted. The need to reach agreement mobilizes their resources, and so they sharpen their intellectual activity and their capacity for interaction. Although reciprocal adjustments are being made, it seems that the children are also coming to view, in some kind of perspective, interpersonal relations between dyads as well as the interactive process itself from a certain distance. They thus objectivize their knowledge of human reactions and the impact the reactions may have on the behavior of others, but also their knowledge of procedures and strategies that make agreement possible. These hypotheses seem all the more plausible seeing that interindividual relations dominate the scenarios created by the children.

Psychosocial Knowledge in the Development Phase

What is striking in the scenes improvised by pairs of children is the coherence of the storyline. The cognitive means that permit this coherence have been analyzed elsewhere (Stambak & Royon, 1985); here the focus is on the content of the scenes in order to understand the social universe as viewed by the children.

The specifically theatrical quality of puppet shows influences content and development. The themes chosen should be entertaining for the audience and the story should be lively enough to prevent boredom. With just two of them in the theater, each manipulating at least one puppet, the children portray the various relationships pursued by the characters represented by the puppets, thereby reflecting the children's own preoccupations. The psychosocial ideas that may accordingly be inferred from the content of the scenes concern more particularly the dynamics of interpersonal relations with their theatrical characteristics already underlined by Forbes et al. (1986). The characters introduced are for the most part human. Their roles then differ according to whether their status is similar or not. Between children and adults, relationships are colored by authority, whereas among peers—children or adults—sympathy and friendship prevail. When an animal is introduced as one of the characters, fear between the human being and the animal is generally the main feature of the relationship.

Regarding human relations in adult–child scenes, authority is the dominant trait. This is not surprising at an age when the children are faced with interdictions and social rules imposed by adults.

Far from depicting the exercise of authority in a stereotypical way with emphasis on the asymmetry of the relationship, the children deploy knowledge of a large number of possibles both regarding ways of exercising authority as of reacting to it. Adults are not represented as being invariably overbearing and uncompromising, but as more or less severe, more or less tolerant, and as having to come to terms with the child. The children in these scenes, far from being limited to obedience and submission, demonstrate various ways of resisting authority. Children, it is clear, have fully grasped that power relationships differ with the character of the persons represented and have a finely graded appreciation of adult demands. They have well integrated the interdictions and moral laws that should be respected and accept submission to them, but when it comes to rules of behavior and good manners they are just as capable of using them to appease authority as of resisting it with a view to evasion.

The subtlety with which the children portray the power structure proves that they analyze their social environment in fine detail, and derive varied knowledge of pertinent characteristics of that environment sufficient to caricature and ridicule the authority relationship.

In another sphere of human relations of which not much notice has been taken in the literature, the children seem greatly interested in life shared by persons of equivalent status (children or adults). When they stage a sympathetic relationship, they show themselves eager to bring out its harmonious character.

In the kindergarten, these children live a collective life sharing the same experiences, events and emotions. When they put on a show they are mainly concerned with identity relations and demonstrate that they take pleasure in bringing out similarity between partners. By means of the characters in the play, who express their satisfaction in sharing actions and rituals, the children portray an affective communion (cf. Wallon, 1949) by imitating the gestures and words of their partner, and make plain their enjoyment in doing so.

The characters staged may express a more intellectual agreement, a sharing of viewpoints on how to go about dealing with third persons. Such an agreement may yield a partnership indulged in to the point of the puppeteers jointly making fun of prevailing values.

The children know that friendly relationships depend on reciprocal confidence that they put to the test by teasing. They show mastery of portraying the friendship of characters who cross one another while making plain that "it's for fun." The oldest children use means to provoke and to disarm their partner while avoiding any breach and reducing aggressive feelings to a minimum. In such scenes, they evince an already well-established knowledge of themselves and of others, and demonstrate their capacity to exploit the particularities of the characters presented for the purpose of teasing.

In scenes dealing with relationships between humans and animals, especially dogs, the children reveal detailed knowledge of wants and attitudes of dogs, but also of the kind of relations that can be entertained with a dog. This animal is shown in fact as a partner whom it is wise to mistrust, for his gentleness alternates with disobedience and although he may at times be submissive he always remains dangerous. The children accordingly use the dog for the purpose of staging fear. Humans who have dealings with dogs may act as masters, companions, trainers, or victims, but, despite this diversity of roles, fear is always present as a kind of permanent caution. Scenes including this animal provide opportunity for the children to practice mastering their fear by exciting it while at the same time defending themselves.

Theatrical pretend play puts children in the privileged position of being able to take up different roles and to react to them. In this situation they can appreciate the position and the proposals of their partner in a variety of perspectives and from different points of view. We thus agree with authors who like Garvey (1982), Bretherton (1984), Wolf (1982), and Forbes et al. (1986) maintained that pretend play, in particular the playing of roles, enhances insight into the behavior and reactions of others.

In our view, the specifically theatrical quality of puppet shows accelerates the construction of such knowledge. This chapter has shown how the children manifest their awareness of the fictional character of the scenes. They are cognizant of the arbitrary aspect of theatrical performance and know that the scenes they invent exist as entities that can be replayed and in which the actors may interchange their roles. In this way, during their very performance, children have the opportunity of detaching themselves even further from the psychosocial reality that is the theme of their scenarios. The distance taken from the content of the improvised scenes undoubtedly contributes to the psychosocial knowledge they are in the course of constructing. One cannot help but suspect that such instances of becoming aware contribute to the management of interpersonal relationships in real life.

As a whole, the data analyzed in this chapter entitle us to assert that children, while negotiating among themselves for agreement on a story to be pursued together, while elaborating scenes in which characters interact in multiple ways, and while simply performing in the theatrical mode evince different kinds of psychosocial knowledge concerning themselves, other people, interpersonal relationships and strategies designed to transform such relations. To condense the totality of our observations it might be said that in pretend play children show their desire to display knowledge of what the self and the other have, and do not have, in common, and that they are in the course of learning that the other is at once similar to and different from the self.

The question that needs to be asked is: In improvising their scenes, do the children merely make use of already acquired knowledge or are they constructing new knowledge? The study of our subjects' performance of puppet shows with their various constraints allows us to argue that the children are in fact engaged in working out new strategies and that these strategies influence the construction of their thought. Some of their lines do appear to be improvisations resulting from the constraints of the here and now, rather than being simply the application of preexisting knowledge.

In the example of the two age-different partners who in consequence have different theatrical abilities, the older child, despite the obstacles she encounters and the difficulties she has to overcome in order to make herself understood, constructs knowledge concerning the understanding and adaptive capacities of a child younger than herself. It may be said that this example results in a double apprenticeship: The younger learns to elaborate puppet shows and the older learns to adapt to the different abilities of a younger child.

So it may be said that, through shared play, children succeed in structuring their social universe while at the same time consolidating and exteriorizing their already existing knowledge. What is more, shared pretend play obliges the children to view reality with a certain detachment which in turn favors reflection on their actions. Such detachment seems to us much more difficult to realize when it comes to actions of everyday life.

No doubt it is the analysis of the interactive processes leading up to the performance of coherent scenes that gives the most convincing results regarding the constructive contribution of shared pretend play: The children negotiate, take their partner's view into account, clarify their intentions, argue, and justify their actions. These interpersonal coordinations, in our view, play as important a part in general psychological development as the intrapersonal coordinations brought to the fore by Piaget.

It is on this note that we close the chapter, underlining how much these occasions for shared pretend play contribute structurally to the development of young children. It has been seen in our study how the children are brought to reflect on the social world and to jointly construct certain quanta of psychosocial knowledge. From another point of view, as other authors have pointed out, shared symbolic activities allow the children to sharpen their reasoning powers, to develop communicative skills, especially language, to enrich their imagination, and to express and master their emotions. Collective pretend play, because of its many-sided richness, appears to us as an activity of high value. Because it is carried out by more than one child and because it leads to equilibrated exchanges, the children evince, consolidate, elaborate, and construct their knowledge at the same time as they sharpen their communicative skills. Situations that favor such social interaction are of the kind that may lead to processes of co-construction. This study thus helps to underpin our constructivist and interactional theory according to which children learn through equilibrated exchanges. It should encourage educators to multiply and diversify such situations (different ages, different partners, different contents) with the aim of ensuring the active engagement of all children in the learning process and in the increase of knowledge, thus contributing to the prevention of marginalization.

ACKNOWLEDGMENTS

We are grateful to the children in day-care centers and kindergartens of the 13th *arrondissement* in Paris for their inventive play and to the staff for their valuable collaboration.

References

Bateson, G. (1955). A theory of play and fantasy. *Psychiatric Research Reports, 2*, 39–51.

Bonica, L. (1986, September). *The role of human similarity in the development of psycho-social competence.* Paper presented at the second European conference on Developmental Psychology, Rome.

Bonica, L. (1987). Procédés de régulation sociale entre enfants de douze mois à trois ans, en situation de jeu. In CRESAS, *On n'apprend pas tout seul* (pp. 67–69). Paris: Editions Sociales Françaises.

Bréauté, M., Ballion, M., Rayna, S., Stambak, M., Joly, A.-M., Lemarchand, Th., Pieronne, F., Cassius, O., & Ansallem, M.-F. (1987). *Au jardin d'enfants, des enfants marionnettistes.* Paris: L'Harmattan.

Brenner, J., & Mueller, E. (1982). Shared meaning in boy toddlers' peer relations. *Child Development, 53*(2), 380–391.

Bretherton, I. (1984). Representing the social world in symbolic play: Reality and fantasy. In I. Bretherton (Ed.), *Symbolic play* (pp. 3–41). New York: Academic Press.

Bruner, J. S. (1972). Nature and uses of immaturity. *American Psychologist, 27*, 687–702.

Butterworth, G. (1991). Editorial preface: Theory of mind. *British Journal of Developmental Psychology, 9*, 1–4.

CRESAS. (1981). *L'échec scolaire n'est pas une fatalité.* Paris: Editions Sociales Françaises.

CRESAS. (1987). *On n'apprend pas tout seul: interactions sociales et constructions des savoirs.* Paris: Editions Sociales Françaises.

Darvill, D. (1982). Ecological influences on children's play. *Contributions to Human Development, 6*, 144–153.

Fein, G. (1981). Pretend play in childhood: An integrative view. *Child Development, 52*, 1095–1118.

Fonzi, A., & Negro-Sanzipriano, E. (1975). *La magia della parole: Alla riscoperta della metafora.* Torino: Einaudi.

Forbes, D., Maxwell-Katz, M., & Paul, B. (1986). "Frame talk:" A dramatic analysis of children's fantasy play. In E. Mueller & C. Cooper (Eds.), *Process and outcome in peer-relationships* (pp. 249–265). New York: Academic Press.

115

Franklin, M. (1981). *Play as the creation of imaginary situations.* Paper presented at the conference on developmental psychology. The 1980's: Werner's influence on theory and practice. Clark University, Worcester, MA.

Garvey, C. (1982). Communication and the development of social role play. In D. Forbes & M. Greenberg (Eds.), *New directions in child development* (pp. 81–101). San Francisco: Jossey-Bass.

Garvey, C., & Berndt, R. (1977). Organization of pretend play. *Catalogue of Selected Documents on Psychology, 7,* 15–89.

Giffin, H. (1984). The coordination of meaning in the creation of a shared make-believe reality. In I. Bretherton (Ed.), *Symbolic play* (pp. 73–101). London: Academic Press.

Golomb, C., & Cornelius, C. B. (1977). Symbolic play and its cognitive significance. *Developmental Psychology, 13,* 246–252.

Grice, H. P. (1975). Logic and conversation. In P. Cole & L. J. Morgan (Eds.), *Syntax and semantics* (Vol. 3, pp. 41–58). New York: Academic Press.

Hutt, J. S., Tyler, S., Hutt, C., & Christophersen, H. (1989). *Play exploration and learning: a natural history of the pre-school.* London: Routledge.

McCune-Nicolich, L. (1981). Toward symbolic functioning: structure of early pretend games and potential parallels with language. *Child Development, 52,* 785–797.

Mead, G. H. (1934). *Mind, self and society.* Chicago: University of Chicago Press.

Moore, R., & Young, D. (1979). Childhood outdoors: Towards a social ecology of the landscape. In I. Altman & J. Wohlwill (Eds.), *Children and environment* (pp. 83–130). New York: Plenum Press.

Musatti, T. (1983). Echanges dans une situation de jeux de "faire semblant" In M. Stambak, M. Barrière, L. Bonica, R. Maisonnet, T. Musatti, S. Rayna, & M. Verba, *Les bébés entre eux* (pp. 93–134). Paris: Presses Universitaires de France.

Musatti, T., & Mayer, S. (1987). Object substitution: Its nature and function. *Human Development, 30,* 225–235.

Musatti, T., & Panni, S. (1981). Social behavior and interaction among daycare center toddlers. *Early Child Development and Care, 7,* 5–25.

Nelson, K., & Seidman, S. (1984). Playing with scripts. In I. Bretherton (Ed.), *Symbolic play* (pp. 45–71). London: Academic Press.

Opie, I., & Opie, P. (1959). *The lore and language of schoolchildren.* London: Oxford University Press.

Orsolini, M. (1987, May). *Narrazione e gioco simbolico.* Paper presented at the international meetung "Il bambino e i simboli," Pistoïa.

Osorina, M. V. (1986). Modern children's lore as an object of interdisciplinary study (Toward an ethnography of childhood). *Soviet Psychology, 3,* 55–76.

Piaget, J. (1923). *Le langage et la pensée chez l'enfant* (3rd enlarged edition, 1948). Neuchâtel, Paris: Delachaux & Niestlé. English edition (1959): *The language and thought of the child.* London: Routledge & Kegan Paul.

Piaget, J. (1926). *La représentation du monde chez l'enfant.* Paris: Alcan. English edition (1929): *The child's conception of the world.* London: Kegan Paul, Trench, Trubner.

Piaget, J. (1932). *Le jugement moral chez l'enfant.* Paris: Alcan. English edition (1932): *The moral judgment of the child.* London: Kegan Paul, Trench, Trubner.

Piaget, J. (1937). *La construction du réel chez l'enfant.* Neuchâtel, Paris: Delachaux & Niestlé. English edition (1954): *The construction of reality in the child.* New York: Basic Books.

Piaget, J. (1945). *La formation du symbole chez l'enfant.* Neuchâtel, Paris: Delachaux & Niestlé. English edition (1951): *Play, dreams and imitation in childhood.* New York: Norton.

Piaget, J. (1965a). *Etudes sociologiques.* Geneva: Droz.

Piaget, J. (1965b). *Sagesse et illusions de la philosophie.* Paris: Presses Universitaires de France. English edition (1971): *Insights and illusions of philosophy.* New York: World Publishing.

Piaget, J. (1976a). L'individualité en histoire. *Revue Européenne des sciences sociales, 14,* 81–123. (Original work published 1963)

Piaget, J. (1976b). Problèmes de la psychosociologie de l'enfance. *Revue Européenne des sciences sociales, 14*, 161–197. (Original work published 1963)

Pontecorvo, C. (1987). *Interactions sociocognitives et acquisition des connaissances en situation scolaire: Contexte théorique, bilan et perspectives.* ISSBD European Congress, Rome, September 1986.

Schwartzman, H. B. (1978). *Transformations: The anthropology of children's play.* New York: Plenum Press.

Sinclair, H., Stambak, M., Lézine, I., Rayna, S., & Verba, M. (1982). *Les bébés et les choses.* Paris: Presses Universitaires de France. English edition (1989): *Infants and objects.* San Diego: Academic Press.

Stambak, M. (1988). Recherche-action et connaissance des processus de construction des connaissances. In M. A. Hugon & C. Seibel (Eds.), *Recherches impliquées, recherches-action: le cas de l'éducation* (pp. 105–107). Paris: De Boek.

Stambak, M., Ballion, M., Bréauté, M., & Rayna, S. (1985). Pretend play and interaction in young children. In R. A. Hinde, A. N. Perret-Clermont, & J. Stevenson-Hinde (Eds.), *Social relationships and cognitive development* (pp. 131–148). Oxford: Oxford University Press.

Stambak, M., Barrière, M., Bonica, L., Maisonnet, R., Musatti, T., Rayna, S., & Verba, M. (1983). *Les bébés entre eux.* Paris: Presses Universitaires de France.

Stambak, M. & Royon, Ch. (1985). Etude de l'organisation d'activités communes chez des enfants de moins de quatre ans. *Archives de Psychologie, 53*, 77–90.

Stambak, M., & Verba, M. (1986). Ecological approach in peer relations: organization of social play. In E. Mueller & C. Cooper (Eds.), *Process and outcome in peer-relationships* (pp. 229–247). New York: Academic Press.

Stockinger-Forys, S. K. & McCune-Nicolich, L. (1984). Shared pretend: Sociodramatic play at 3 years of age. In I. Bretherton (Ed.), *Symbolic play* (pp. 159–191). London: Academic Press.

Verba, M. (1982). Contribution à l'étude de la communication préverbale entre enfants. *Bulletin d'Audiophonologie, 2–3*, 142–159.

Verba, M. (1985, May). *Construction interindividuelle des jeux de fiction chez les jeunes enfants.* Paper presented at the third Journées du groupe francophone d'étude du développement psychologique de l'enfant jeune, Nice.

Verba, M. (1987a). Constructions interactives chez les jeunes enfants: Apport des enfants plus âgés dans le groupe. In CRESAS, *On n'apprend pas tout seul* (pp. 91–94). Paris: Editions Sociales Françaises.

Verba, M. (1987b, April). *Co-operation, tutoring and imitation in social symbolic play: The role of the older child.* Paper presented at the eighth biennial SRCD Congress, Baltimore, MD.

Verba, M., & Isambert, A. L. (1987). La costruzione delle conoscenze attraverso gli scambi tra bambini. In I. Bondiolo, A. Mantovanni & S. Mantovanni (Eds.), *Manuale critico dell' asilo nido* (pp. 306–323). Milan: Franco Angeli.

Verba, M., Stambak, M., & Sinclair, H. (1982). Physical knowledge and social interaction in children aged 12–18 months. In G. Forman (Ed.), *Action and thought* (pp. 267–296). New York: Academic Press.

Vygotsky, L. (1967). Play and its role in the mental development of the child. *Soviet Psychology, 5*, 6–18.

Wallon, H. (1949). *Les origines du caractère chez l'enfant.* Paris: Presses Universitaires de France.

Watzlawick, P., Beavin, H. J., & Jackson, D. (1967). *The pragmatics of human communication.* New York: Norton.

Wolf, D. (1982). Understanding others: A longitudinal case study of the concept of independent agency. In G. Forman (Ed.), *Action and thought* (pp. 297–325). New York: Academic Press.

Author Index

A

Ansallem, M.-F., *115*

B

Ballion, M., 79, *115*, *117*
Barrière, M., *116*, *117*
Bateson, G., xiv, xvi, xvii, 56, *115*
Beavin, H. J., 56, *117*
Berndt, R., 2, 27, 83, *116*
Bonica, L., 57, 109, *115*, *116*, *117*
Bréauté, M., 79, 81, 97, *115*, *117*
Brenner, J., 2, *115*
Bretherton, I., 1, 89, 112, *115*
Bruner, J. S., xi, *115*
Butterworth, G., xvi, *115*

C

Cassius, O., *115*
Christophersen, H., 1, *116*
Cornelius, C. B., xvii, *116*

D

Darvill, D., 31, *115*

F

Fein, G., 1, 5, *115*
Fonzi, A., 75, *115*
Forbes, D., xvi, 2, 8, 83, 89, 110, 112, *115*
Franklin, M., 2, *116*

G

Garvey, C., 2, 4, 5, 27, 54, 83, 89, 112, *116*
Giffin, H., 2, 5, 25, 70, 83, *116*
Golomb, C., xvii, *116*
Grice, H. P., xii, *116*

H

Hutt, C., 1, *116*
Hutt, J. S., 1, *116*

Subject Index

A

Abstraction, viii
Academic failure, 80
Age difference in puppet shows, 85–87, 109, 112–113
Animals, 17–19, 27, 65–67, 89, 92, 102–105, 110, 111
Authority, xiii, 88, 89, 90–96, 105–107, 109, 110, 111

C

Causality, viii, 36, 51, 53
  magico-phenomenist, 36
Child folklore, 54
Communication,
  ambiguous, 55, 61, 68–71, 73, 76
  block, 58, 59, 61, 72, 73, 74, 76, 109
  in-frame/out-of-frame, 5, 8, 19, 24–25, 60, 61, 63, 88
  levels of, xiv, xv, 56–58, 61, 64, 66, 70, 74–75
  rules of, 71, 73
  verbal/nonverbal, x, xiv, 1, 2, 5, 7, 8, 56–58, 69

Complicity, 97, 98, 99, 101
Conflict, xv, xvi, 4, 40, 96
  and resolution of conflict, 55–77
  avoiding, 88, 109
  sociocognitive, 83
Confrontation, xvi, 28, 80
Conservation, permanence,
  of liquids and substance, xvii
  of personal identity, xvii
  of propositions, xiii
  of scenes, themes, xvii, 107
Constructivism, vii, viii, 80, 113
Conventionalization of symbolism, 53, 54

D

Dead-end dialogue, 23
Detachment from immediate situation, viii, ix, x, xi, 112, 113
Development,
  cognitive, xi, xvii, 28, 52, 54, 113
  language, xi, 113
  social, 52, 79, 113
Double bind, paradoxical injunction, 57, 63–65, 72, 74